BOB MARLEY

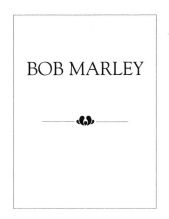

BOB MARLEY

Sean Dolan

CHELSEA HOUSE PUBLISHERS
Philadelphia

Chelsea House Publishers

Editorial Director	Richard Rennert
Production Manager	Pamela Loos
Art Director	Sara Davis
Picture Editor	Judy Hasday

Staff for BOB MARLEY

Senior Editors	Philip Koslow, Jane Shumate
Associate Editor	Therese De Angelis
Editorial Assistant	Kristine Brennan
Designer	Alison Burnside
Picture Researcher	Ellen Barrett Dudley
Cover Illustrator	Richard Leonard

Library of Congress Cataloging-in-Publication Data
Dolan, Sean.
    Bob Marley / by Sean Dolan.
       p. cm.—(Black Americans of achievement)
    Includes bibliographical references and index.
Summary: Traces the life of the Jamaican musician who helped
popularize reggae before his untimely death.
ISBN 0-7910-2041-X
    0-7910-3255-8 (pbk.)
1. Marley, Bob—Juvenile literature. 2. Singers—Jamaica—
Biography—Juvenile literature. 3. Reggae musicians—Jamaica—
Biography—Juvenile literature. [1. Marley, Bob. 2. Musicians.
3. Blacks—Jamaica—Biography. 4. Reggae music.] I. Title
ML420.M329D6 1996
782.42164—dc20
[B]
                     95-35932
                     CIP
                     AC MN

CONTENTS

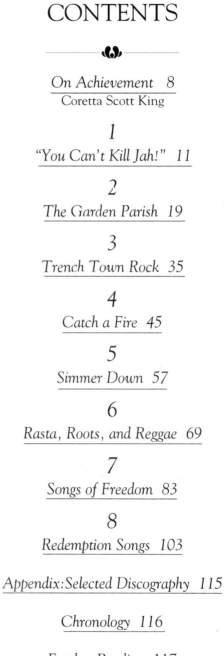

BLACK AMERICANS OF ACHIEVEMENT

HENRY AARON
baseball great

KAREEM ABDUL-JABBAR
basketball great

ALVIN AILEY
choreographer

MUHAMMAD ALI
heavyweight champion

RICHARD ALLEN
*religious leader and
social activist*

MAYA ANGELOU
author

LOUIS ARMSTRONG
musician

ARTHUR ASHE
tennis great

JOSEPHINE BAKER
entertainer

JAMES BALDWIN
author

BENJAMIN BANNEKER
scientist and mathematician

AMIRI BARAKA
poet and playwright

COUNT BASIE
bandleader and composer

ROMARE BEARDEN
artist

JAMES BECKWOURTH
frontiersman

MARY MCLEOD BETHUNE
educator

JULIAN BOND
civil rights leader and politician

GWENDOLYN BROOKS
poet

JIM BROWN
football great

STOKELY CARMICHAEL
civil rights leader

GEORGE WASHINGTON
CARVER
botanist

RAY CHARLES
musician

CHARLES CHESNUTT
author

JOHN COLTRANE
musician

BILL COSBY
entertainer

PAUL CUFFE
merchant and abolitionist

COUNTEE CULLEN
poet

BENJAMIN DAVIS, SR.,
AND BENJAMIN DAVIS, JR.
military leaders

MILES DAVIS
musician

FATHER DIVINE
religious leader

FREDERICK DOUGLASS
abolitionist editor

CHARLES DREW
physician

W. E. B. DU BOIS
scholar and activist

PAUL LAURENCE DUNBAR
poet

KATHERINE DUNHAM
dancer and choreographer

DUKE ELLINGTON
bandleader and composer

RALPH ELLISON
author

JULIUS ERVING
basketball great

JAMES FARMER
civil rights leader

ELLA FITZGERALD
singer

MARCUS GARVEY
black nationalist leader

JOSH GIBSON
baseball great

DIZZY GILLESPIE
musician

WHOOPI GOLDBERG
entertainer

ALEX HALEY
author

PRINCE HALL
social reformer

JIMI HENDRIX
musician

MATTHEW HENSON
explorer

CHESTER HIMES
author

BILLIE HOLIDAY
singer

LENA HORNE
entertainer

LANGSTON HUGHES
poet

ZORA NEALE HURSTON
author

JESSE JACKSON
civil rights leader and politician

MICHAEL JACKSON
entertainer

JACK JOHNSON
heavyweight champion

JAMES WELDON JOHNSON
author

MAGIC JOHNSON
basketball great

SCOTT JOPLIN
composer

BARBARA JORDAN
politician

MICHAEL JORDAN
basketball great

CORETTA SCOTT KING
civil rights leader

MARTIN LUTHER KING, JR.
civil rights leader

LEWIS LATIMER
scientist

SPIKE LEE
filmmaker

CARL LEWIS
champion athlete

JOE LOUIS
heavyweight champion

RONALD MCNAIR
astronaut

MALCOLM X
militant black leader

THURGOOD MARSHALL
Supreme Court justice

TONI MORRISON
author

ELIJAH MUHAMMAD
religious leader

EDDIE MURPHY
entertainer

JESSE OWENS
champion athlete

SATCHEL PAIGE
baseball great

CHARLIE PARKER
musician

GORDON PARKS
photographer

ROSA PARKS
civil rights leader

SIDNEY POITIER
actor

ADAM CLAYTON POWELL, JR.
political leader

COLIN POWELL
military leader

LEONTYNE PRICE
opera singer

A. PHILIP RANDOLPH
labor leader

PAUL ROBESON
singer and actor

JACKIE ROBINSON
baseball great

DIANA ROSS
entertainer

BILL RUSSELL
basketball great

JOHN RUSSWURM
publisher

SOJOURNER TRUTH
antislavery activist

HARRIET TUBMAN
antislavery activist

NAT TURNER
slave revolt leader

DENMARK VESEY
slave revolt leader

ALICE WALKER
author

MADAM C. J. WALKER
entrepreneur

BOOKER T. WASHINGTON
educator

IDA WELLS BARNETT
civil rights leader

WALTER WHITE
civil rights leader

OPRAH WINFREY
entertainer

STEVIE WONDER
musician

RICHARD WRIGHT
author

ON
ACHIEVEMENT

———— ✿ ————

Coretta Scott King

Before you begin this book, I hope you will ask yourself what the word *excellence* means to you. I think that it's a question we should all ask, and keep asking as we grow older and change. Because the truest answer to it should never change. When you think of excellence, perhaps you think of success at work; or of becoming wealthy; or meeting the right person, getting married, and having a good family life.

Those important goals are worth striving for, but there is a better way to look at excellence. As Martin Luther King, Jr., said in one of his last sermons, "I want you to be first in love. I want you to be first in moral excellence. I want you to be first in generosity. If you want to be important, wonderful. If you want to be great, wonderful. But recognize that he who is greatest among you shall be your servant."

My husband, Martin Luther King, Jr., knew that the true meaning of achievement is service. When I met him, in 1952, he was already ordained as a Baptist preacher and was working toward a doctoral degree at Boston University. I was studying at the New England Conservatory and dreamed of accomplishments in music. We married a year later, and after I graduated the following year we moved to Montgomery, Alabama. We didn't know it then, but our notions of achievement were about to undergo a dramatic change.

You may have read or heard about what happened next. What began with the boycott of a local bus line grew into a national movement, and by the time he was assassinated in 1968 my husband had fashioned a black movement powerful enough to shatter forever the practice of racial segregation. What you may not have read about is where he got his method for resisting injustice without compromising his religious beliefs.

He adopted the strategy of nonviolence from a man of a different race, who lived in a different country, and even practiced a different religion. The man was Mahatma Gandhi, the great leader of India, who devoted his life to serving humanity in the spirit of love and nonviolence. It was in these principles that Martin discovered his method for social reform. More than anything else, those two principles were the key to his achievements.

This book is about black Americans who served society through the excellence of their achievements. It forms a part of the rich history of black men and women in America—a history of stunning accomplishments in every field of human endeavor, from literature and art to science, industry, education, diplomacy, athletics, jurisprudence, even polar exploration.

Not all of the people in this history had the same ideals, but I think you will find something that all of them had in common. Like Martin Luther King, Jr., they all decided to become "drum majors" and serve humanity. In that principle—whether it was expressed in books, inventions, or song—they found something outside themselves to use as a goal and a guide. Something that showed them a way to serve others, instead of only living for themselves.

Reading the stories of these courageous men and women not only helps us discover the principles that we will use to guide our own lives but also teaches us about our black heritage and about America itself. It is crucial for us to know the heroes and heroines of our history and to realize that the price we paid in our struggle for equality in America was dear. But we must also understand that we have gotten as far as we have partly because America's democratic system and ideals made it possible.

We are still struggling with racism and prejudice. But the great men and women in this series are a tribute to the spirit of our democratic ideals and the system in which they have flourished. And that makes their stories special and worth knowing. ❧

1

"YOU CAN'T KILL JAH!"

— ❧ —

THE PROPHET WAS silent as they drove him down the mountainside. For almost two whole days now his whereabouts had been a secret, the subject of frenzied rumor and intense speculation. He was dead, the people mourned, a victim of assassins' bullets. No, others insisted, he was in hiding, protected by his power and guarded by the faithful, and he would reappear to the people when the time was right, for you cannot kill Jah (God) or his messenger. He was hiding in the mountains with the rich men he knew; no, he had sought refuge among the poor, humble "sufferers" in Trench Town, the only people he could trust. The government had set him up, maybe even orchestrated the shooting; no, no, it was the opposition party, maybe in league with the CIA. He was wounded; he was unharmed. He was safe; he was dead. He would appear tonight and prophesy for the people; no, he was gone, into exile in England or Florida, on some other island or in some safer place than the tortured paradise of Jamaica.

Beside the prophet in the backseat of the red Volvo, the police commissioner opened a small briefcase. Removing the components of a submachine gun, he quickly assembled the weapon. The officer in the passenger seat in front did the same, as did those riding in the other vehicles in the swiftly moving motorcade. Just in case, the commissioner

Bob Marley, who is remembered as a "musical prophet," mesmerized audiences with his intense performances. His mother recalls how concertgoers could "see he [was] singing from the depths of his heart. . . . because he was under such a glorious sensation of the spirit that you could see it just flowing."

assured the still-silent prophet, who was now wearing his famous "screwface." Do not mess with me, the screwface said, a sometimes necessary protection for one besieged from dawn to dusk by those asking something from him—words, music, strength, advice, attention, money, inspiration, love. "He would wear a screwface to keep people away," a friend explained. "When you are pure in heart, you can feel when impurity comes near you. The spirits don't mesh." Another friend agreed. "Him only shield he could wear was him noted screwface," this man recalled, using the creative syntax of the Jamaican patois. It was a means of self-protection familiar to his fellow sufferers, learned from hard times and hard knocks at the hands of the "downpressers." The prophet was "born screw," his wife, Rita, once said. "Him not have to make it up."

Enemies and friends alike were wary of the screwface; its wearer, after all, was believed by some to possess strange powers. Small, seemingly slight, soft-spoken, the prophet, it was said, yet feared no man or spirit. He was both the Tuff Gong, willing and able to give as good as he got in the cutthroat world of the Kingston ghetto, and the Duppy Conqueror, communicant with the spirits and phantoms of the shadow world. With good reason, many people regarded him as the most powerful— and possibly the most threatening—man in Jamaica. Within a few short years, he would be called "the most dangerous black man in the world."

The screwface was impossible to read. Was it suspicion or trust that held sway behind the unspeaking mask? Courage or fear or simple exhaustion? Did he believe that he was safe in this motorcade, guarded by government ministers and officers, or that he was being led to the slaughter? They had used him before, and he had the bandaged but still throbbing bullet wounds on his chest and arm to show for it. His wife, her own head bandaged where a bullet had grazed her skull, had begged him not to go with these men down the mountain. Frightened, his closest friends had scattered and were incommunicado in various hideaways.

In front, the radio crackled. One of the prophet's guards spoke into a walkie-talkie, then listened intently and relayed the information to him. The crowd at the National Heroes Circle Stadium in Kingston, their destination, was growing by the minute. Rumors that the prophet's appearance had been canceled, even that he was dead, had not discouraged the people. By four o'clock that afternoon, 50,000 spectators had already gathered at the stadium. The crowd had now swelled to between 80,000 and 100,000. The screwface gave no sign that it had heard.

Outside the window of the automobile, a gentle Jamaican December night was softly falling as the motorcade wound its way down the mountainside. In the slowly gathering dusk, firelight flickered here and there, leaping upward from rusty metal barrels and stacks of recently gathered scrapwood—the bonfires around which the sufferers gathered to cook, to socialize, to talk, to sing, to remember the other nights they had spent like this, and to remind one another to "no cry." Many nights had the prophet spent like this, around the fire "with the good people we meet." With them, he had not worn the screwface. Then he had smiled in his soft way and laughed and sang with them all as his friend Georgie "made the fire light," the "logwood burnin'" through the night" until at last he would go to bed alone on a wood table in a cold corner of a friend's kitchen. He was one of them, the sufferers knew; even death could never take him from them. "Cold cold ground was my bed last night, and rockstone was my pillow," the prophet sang to and of the sufferers; "them bellyful, but we hungry."

Now fire glinted behind the window of the automobile as the prophet lit a spliff of ganja (marijuana). For himself and the other believers of his religion, Rastafarianism, ganja was not a drug but a sacrament, its use sanctioned by the Bible and nature. A gift from Jah to the downpressed, ganja acted as an aid to meditation and reasoning and as an instrument of peacefulness and joy. The prophet inhaled rapidly and deeply as the commissioner and his officers pretended that nothing out of the ordinary was taking place. For the first time that night, the screwface was relaxed.

Then the line of cars slowed, and the screwface returned. This was not the National Heroes Circle Stadium. Here the fires burned brighter, and mobs of people flooded the street, surrounding the cars, rocking them, peering through the windows. Huge bonfires blazed, and amplified dance music crackled through tinny loudspeakers. This was enemy territory, the prophet immediately realized, the stronghold of the Jamaica Labour Party (JLP), the opposition party in the violently contested upcoming national elections. Somehow, the motorcade had blundered into a JLP "garrison" in the midst of an election rally.

"JLP War Zone" proclaimed the brightly colored letters on the neighborhood's cinderblock walls, and that was no exaggeration. The ghettos of Kingston were divided into numerous such garrisons, each of them claimed and controlled by gunmen loyal to the two rival political parties, the JLP and the People's National Party (PNP). In the ghettos, where most of Jamaica's voters resided, the parties fought for allegiance, buying loyalty with jobs, housing, and handouts, and enforcing it at the barrel of a gun. Party loyalty in Jamaica was almost akin to religious faith, and national elections were contested in an atmosphere just short of outright civil war. To back the wrong party could cost one one's job, one's house, even one's life. The "ranking" gunmen

of each party became celebrities in their own right, powerful figures revered as Robin Hoods by their followers, reviled as gangsters and terrorists by their opponents. The ongoing 1976 election campaign had already been the bloodiest in Jamaica's history, with several hundred people dying in election-related violence.

The intrusion of a government motorcade into their garrison was not received warmly by the JLP faithful. They swarmed around the vehicles, undeterred by the sight of police uniforms or the sirens whirring on the vehicles' roofs, slowing the cars' progress to a crawl, then a complete halt. They peered inside the windows, trying to learn who it was that had dared breech their stronghold.

Those inside the vehicles were not much happier. Was it a mistake that had brought them here or more "poli-tricks," as the sufferers called it, of the same kind that had got the prophet and his wife and friends shot up in their home two nights earlier? That had clearly been a setup of some kind, when

Gunmen protect Jamaica Labour Party candidate Edward Seaga (right, behind rifleman) as guards escort him across a West Kingston street. Jamaican political campaigns are fiercely waged, and in 1976 several hundred people died from election-related violence.

the guards appointed by the government to patrol around the house strangely disappeared just a short time before gunmen burst in and began firing. Only Jah had allowed his prophet to survive. Was he now being delivered up to his enemies, handed over for elimination, by his self-proclaimed friends in the PNP, whose integrity he had good cause to mistrust? Was the botched assassination now to be finished off properly? "Jesus, this is an ambush," thought one of the prophet's friends, who was riding in a car behind the red Volvo, as the motorcade came to a stop.

Chanting campaign slogans, the surging crowd seemed only to grow larger and more agitated. What thoughts the screwface hid then are unknown, for in

Bloodied and shaken, Marley awaits treatment at a Kingston hospital after being shot in the chest and left arm by unknown assailants.

the dusk and firelight he had been recognized. Beside him, the police commissioner went unnoticed, but there was no mistaking the identity of the man with the untamed lion's mane of dreadlocks, the wispy growth of beard on the chin and lower jaw, the light brown skin, the deep-set, dark, soulful eyes, the prideful carriage, and the indomitable air that seemed to proclaim, as he had once said about himself: "I don't come to bow. I come to conquer." Yes, the prophet was alive and well within, the most revered—and feared—man in all of Jamaica halted at this garrison roadblock.

In an instant, the identity of the passenger spread through the crowd, his name whispered at first, like a curse or a blessing—in either circumstance something too sacred or powerful to be uttered aloud. It traveled to the outermost fringes of the crowd and then, like a wave gathering momentum as it speeds toward the shore, returned inward, gaining in power and volume as the onlookers, as if collectively obeying some unspoken order, parted to let the motorcade pass. As they did so, they called out his name, the solidarity of the sufferers, for this moment at least, overpowering the partisan call of poli-tricks.

"Bob Mar-ley! Bob Mar-ley! Bob Mar-ley!" they chanted over and over again, and the screwface dissolved into a gentle smile, then laughter.

The cheers of the crowd receded as the motorcade rolled onward, only to be replaced by a deeper roar, heard first through the crackling static on the walkie-talkie and then outside, all around them, filling the night. They were approaching the National Heroes Circle Stadium, and the huge throng there had just heard an official announcement from the stage: Bob Marley was not only alive but was just minutes away. The prophet would, as originally promised, sing for the people that evening. ❧

2

THE GARDEN PARISH

❧

NESTA ROBERT MARLEY was born on February 6, 1945, in the hamlet of Camden Hall, which is located in the mountainous country of the parish of St. Ann, in the north-central part of Jamaica. To residents of the island—which lies south of the eastern end of Cuba and due west of Haiti—St. Ann is the "garden parish," renowned for its fertile land, natural beauty, and strong-minded, independent inhabitants. For black Jamaicans, it holds special significance as the birthplace of the island's two most prominent heroes, Bob Marley and Marcus Garvey. In the early part of the 20th century, Garvey earned great fame, as well as political persecution, as an advocate of black self-determination and the "back to Africa" movement. As such, and especially for his supposed prediction that blacks should look to Africa for the imminent crowning of a new king who would bring redemption, Garvey is regarded by Rastas as second in importance only to Haile Selassie (1892–1975), the former Ethiopian emperor considered to be the Messiah himself. Garvey's prophet's mantle would be inherited by Bob Marley.

Fittingly for one who would offer his "songs of freedom" as redemption for Jamaica's black sufferers, Marley's mixed ancestry embodied his homeland's tormented colonial past. Until 1962 Jamaica was ruled by Great Britain, whose formidable mariners

The lush, rolling hillside of St. Ann Parish was Marley's first home.

19

had driven the Spanish from the island in 1655. The Spanish claim to Jamaica had been based on Christopher Columbus's discovery of the island in 1494, during his second New World voyage. By the time of the Spanish defeat, the island's original inhabitants, the peaceful Arawak Indians, had been driven to extinction, eradicated by exposure to Old World diseases to which they had no natural immunity (such as smallpox, measles, and influenza) and by brutal mistreatment at the hands of the Spanish, who enslaved them to clear and tend their fields, build their cabins, and extract the gold and silver from their mines.

Under British rule, Jamaica was initially best known as the "pirate capital" of the Caribbean. From its harbors, buccaneers and privateers—pirates granted official license by the English to prey on foreign shipping—routinely plundered Spanish vessels. Infamous cutthroats such as Bluebeard and Henry Morgan made Port Royal (across the bay from present-day Kingston) notorious as "the most wicked city in Christendom." Morgan even became deputy governor of the island for a time. But the seeming intervention of a biblical act of justice brought the pirate era to a crashing halt in 1692, when a tremendous earthquake plunged much of Port Royal, with its many seedy taverns and brothels, into Kingston Bay. Most of those who survived were felled by the epidemics of typhus and cholera that followed the disaster, and the city was never rebuilt.

By that time the English had discovered another source of wealth from the island's natural bounty. Jamaica's climate and topography made it ideal for the production of sugar, for which Europe and the North American colonies seemed to have an inexhaustible appetite. Indeed, demand for the sweetener was so great that it generated profits akin (in one modern-day historian's estimate) to those available in the cocaine trade today. Along with the other valuable British possessions in the West Indies, Jamaica became one of the "sugar islands," a huge agricultural factory devoted to the cultivation of sugarcane, the refinement of sugar, and its shipment to North America and Europe as part of the incredibly lucrative "triangle trade."

The third part of the triangle lay on the Slave Coast in West Africa, the area bordering the Bight of Benin in the present-day nations of Ghana, Togo, Benin, and Nigeria. In the 17th and 18th centuries, millions of blacks were forcibly brought across the Atlantic from the Slave Coast and other African regions (such as Senegambia and Kongo) to live, work, and die as slaves in Jamaica's sugar fields. Their labor made the island the largest and richest

An Arawak Indian leader greets Christopher Columbus on the island of Cuba in 1492. Two years later Columbus landed on Jamaica, and shortly thereafter the Spanish began enslaving the island's Indians.

sugar producer in the Caribbean; between 1673 and 1740 the number of sugar plantations on Jamaica grew from 57 to 430, and the wealth of the white British planter class on the island increased correspondingly.

Dominant economically, politically, and socially, the elite white governing class was never more than a tiny numerical minority in Jamaica. In 1775, for example, Jamaica was inhabited by 13,000 whites and more than 200,000 blacks, virtually all of them slaves. Today only 4 percent of Jamaica's population of slightly more than 2.5 million people is white, while 91 percent is black or of black ancestry. Their small numbers, combined with the necessity of maintaining the slave system by the threat and use of brute force and terror, instilled in the whites a siege mentality. Nothing scared them more than the prospect of unified black resistance, whether through armed uprisings or political organizing.

Since the time of the Spanish, black resistance commonly meant escape to the wilderness—particularly the rugged Blue Mountains in the east and the impenetrable Cockpit Country, the island's west-central region, whose limestone craters resemble the surface of the moon—and the establishment of self-governing, self-sufficient communities. The runaway slaves, known to the English as Maroons (from the Spanish word *cimarrón*, which means "wild"), became legendary for the ferocity and craftiness with which they defended their hard-won freedom. For roughly 50 years, from 1690 to 1739— a time when the red-coated British army was gaining a reputation as the most formidable fighting force in the world—the Maroons fought the English to a dead standstill. Inspired by their famous leader Cujo, the Mountain Lion, they mastered the art of guerrilla warfare, launching hit-and-run attacks and then melting back into their mountain hideaways,

where even crack British troops were reluctant to follow.

The Maroons' daring exploits forced the British to grant them freedom on their own land, where by treaty neither the British nor the colonial government was to have any legal jurisdiction. However, the whites employed a strategy that would serve them increasingly well in Jamaica over the years: divide and conquer. Aware that a half century of warfare against a great world power had left the Maroon communities exhausted, the British exploited the disdain that the proud, freedom-loving runaways and their descendants felt for those of their countrymen who "allowed" themselves to remain in slavery. By terms of the peace treaty, the Maroons were obligated to help the British "kill, suppress or destroy" all future black rebels and to track down and return to their masters all runaway slaves. Once an inspiration to black Jamaicans, the Maroons now became another feared oppressor.

Black resistance continued nonetheless. A sec-

Slaves perform backbreaking labor on a sugarcane plantation under the watchful eye of a white overseer. During the 17th and 18th centuries, thousands of blacks were forcibly brought from Africa to Jamaica, which emerged as the largest and richest sugar producer in the Caribbean.

ond, smaller-scale Maroon uprising took place in 1795. The rebellious Maroons succeeded in burning the town of Trelawney to the ground but were soon vanquished, with the surviving rebels being shipped into permanent exile in Nova Scotia, Canada. In 1831 a preacher named Sam Sharpe led the last major slave rebellion on Jamaica. It took the authorities six months to restore order. "Rather death than life as a slave" were the last words uttered by Sharpe as he met his end on the gallows in the town of Montego Bay.

Deliverance for the rest of Sharpe's fellow slaves came three years later, in 1834, when the moral arguments of the island's religious leaders, coupled with the mounting conviction that Jamaica would never know peace so long as the slave system existed, brought about emancipation. Initially, freedom for Jamaica's blacks was but a legal formality, as the newly freed slaves were required to work for 40 hours a week for four years for their former masters—for no wages. Finally, in 1838, slavery as a legal institution was officially and genuinely abolished. Relatively few of the former slaves chose to remain on the plantations as contract laborers.

Though the glory days of the Jamaican sugar industry were at an end, the planter class retained economic, political, and social control. Denied the vote and the right to hold political office, blacks had no power to influence the life of the nation. Newly raised from slavery, they lacked the means to obtain land of any significant quantity or quality, the capital to establish themselves in businesses, and access to higher education. Control of the island's wealth and opportunity remained where it always had been, with a small white elite, the descendants of Jamaica's colonial rulers. To this day, over 50 percent of Jamaica's land is owned by fewer than 1,000 individuals, and it remains a truism that the island is ruled by 21 families, all of them of

European descent.

Though not a scion of the 21 families, Bob Marley's father was a member of this ruling class. In 1944 Captain Norval Sinclair Marley of the British West Indian Regiment was appointed overseer of the Crown lands in the parish of St. Ann. As such, his duties involved making periodic inspections, on horseback, of the government's huge landholdings in the remote rural area. The job brought him into regular contact with the people of the parish, on whose hospitality he often relied for shelter and food. Captain Marley often stayed in the large house owned by an elderly black woman named Katherine Malcolm (known to her family as Yaya) in the tiny settlement of Nine Miles, so called because of its distance from St. Ann's Bay.

The tale of the middle-aged British officer and the 17-year-old Cedella Malcolm, Yaya's grand-

During the 18th century, daring runaway slaves called Maroons fiercely defended the independent settlements they had established in isolated areas. This illustration depicts one such settlement at Trelawney Town.

daughter, is, according to the son who was born of their relationship, an old and familiar one on the island. "Like you can read it, you know; it's one o' dem slave stories," Bob Marley would relate years later, with some bitterness. "White guy get the black woman and breed her." On another occasion, he explained, "I'm born in Babylon. My father, a guy who got together with my mother, he's a English. . . a guy who was a captain in the Army, go to war. You can't get no more Babylon than that! You know what I mean?" His mother, Marley asserted with considerable pride, was "African, a black woman from way in St. Ann's, way in Jamaica, way in the country."

Bob Marley would say on many occasions that he was "born fatherless." But when Norval Marley learned that Cedella Malcolm was pregnant, he did not immediately abandon her, as men in his position usually did in such cases. Instead, to the immense surprise of nearly everyone involved, especially his wealthy Kingston family, Marley agreed to marry Malcolm and promised to take care of her and their son. The wedding took place on June 9, 1944, but by that time Marley was having second thoughts about his decision. Immediately before the wedding he informed his bride that he was going away soon—the next day in fact—to Kingston, where he was taking a new job as a foreman on a construction project. Cedella was not to come with him or join him later; his family would not like it. However, he promised to visit her every weekend and provide for the support of his son.

Predictably, Norval made few visits during Cedella's pregnancy, and he appeared even less often once his mother and brother learned of the marriage and threatened to disinherit him. After the birth of the boy, Cedella saw her husband on only a handful of occasions. Norval bestowed the name of Nesta Robert on the seven-pound four-ounce infant—Robert after his brother and Nesta for reasons unexplained. He continued to send money for a brief time, but he visited for only one purpose—to convince Cedella that she should surrender her boy to him to be raised in Kingston.

"Never you ever let him take that child from you," Cedella's father, Omeriah Malcolm, warned. Though poor by the standards of white Jamaicans, living in a crude cabin of plaster and zinc, Omeriah Malcolm was the most prosperous and respected farmer in the Nine Miles region. On his lands high in the mountains he grew coffee, bananas, mangoes, pimientos, oranges, yams, and tangerines, which he hauled to market in a donkey-drawn cart or an old truck. He also owned a small grocery store, a bakery, and a dry-goods store. Descended from the Cromanty people of Ghana, the Malcolms, like several other families in the area, had resided in the vicinity of Nine Miles since the early 17th century, living and working as tenant slaves until emancipation and then helping establish the free village of blacks that even today appears on few maps; it is located far from the area's only paved road, which connects the village of Alexandria and the town of Claremont.

Much more than his farming success and his ancestry made Omeriah Malcolm the most respected citizen of Nine Miles. He was also revered as a *myalman*, a kind of benevolent conjuror or healer trained in the Jamaican folk religion, *kumina*. Just as the patois spoken by Jamaican blacks was English overlaid with numerous African grammatical formulations, usages, and words, so too the religious faith of rural Jamaican blacks was a blend of Christianity and traditional customs, practices, and beliefs deeply rooted in the African heritage of the people.

The most important rituals were those associated with *obeah*, which comes from an African word meaning "magic" or "sorcery." The obeahman used his learning in the magical arts to harness and exploit the powers of the *duppies*, the mischievous, potentially malignant spirits of the dead. As such, the obeahman was a figure of power in the community, someone to be respected, even feared. In the time of the slaves, the obeahman had been the protector of the oppressed, their avenger against the whites; now, more often, he was seen as a malignant influence.

The myalman was a more positive practitioner of the mystic arts. Whereas the obeahman might enlist duppies to inflict harm or even kill someone, the myalman used his learning to counteract such negative influences. The myalman believed that the power of the spirit world should be used only to do good; he knew the curative and magical powers of the infinite variety of herbs and plants that grew in the Jamaican bush, and he could mix them into potions, fashion amulets, and perform rituals that could protect a person from duppies or even old Screwface himself, as rural Jamaicans sometimes called Satan.

When his daughter Cedella became pregnant, Omeriah Malcolm cautioned her to take heed of the Jamaican belief that expectant mothers were particularly vulnerable to the work of malignant spirits. "Always remember," he would say, "you are between life and death until you give birth to that baby." He also taught Cedella which herbs could ease the discomforts of pregnancy and childbirth and which plant leaves were suitable for cleaning the new baby's delicate skin. When little Nesta suddenly took ill at the age of four months, it was Omeriah who concluded that the baby's vomiting and seizures were the work of Screwface. "Somebody science him," he explained, "put duppy on the boy." After consulting with Yaya, his equally knowledgeable mother, Omeriah prepared a potion of nearly a dozen different herbs. When fed to Nesta, the potion quickly caused the illness to lift.

Before long people were noticing that the small, dark-eyed boy had unusual powers of his own. Several qualities set him apart, aside from his light skin tone and white ancestry—neither of which was looked upon with particular favor by the people of Nine Miles, who were extremely proud of their African heritage. There was his quietness, for example; for a boy of four or five, Nesta seemed unusually, even strangely, thoughtful, with a penetrating stare that seemed to be searching for whatever secrets lay hidden beneath the surface appearance of things. Combined with his obvious intelligence, his gaze made adults, even his mother, somewhat uneasy. He seemed to prefer to spend much of his time alone, lost in thought; many were the times that Cedella, walking along some dusty path through the bush to or from the Malcolm fields, would be startled to come upon spindly little barefoot Nesta, sitting contemplatively under a tree or upon some rock. What are you doing, she would ask him, do you not fear the blackheart man? (The blackheart man is an evil spirit, not unlike a bogeyman, who is said by Jamaicans to prey upon disobedient or careless little children.) And always, she said, her son would respond only with "a smile so blue-swee," meaning cunning, knowing, elusive.

Then there was the fortune telling. Cedella was not especially surprised when neighbors began to inform her that they regularly went to Nesta, a child of five, to have their palms read. The boy, they insisted, told them things about themselves that he could not possibly have known, and he made predictions that invariably came true. "The finger of the Lord is upon the boy," his grandfather proclaimed. "Him a manchild with powers that may grow or may fade." It was an opinion that his mother soon came to share, a harbinger of things to come. Looking back years later, she recalled,

> How he do things and prophesy things, he is not just by
> himself—he have higher powers, even from when he is a
> little boy. The way I felt, the kind of vibes I get when Bob
> comes around. . . . It's too honorable. I always look upon
> him with great respect: there is something inside telling
> me that he is not only a son—there is something greater
> in this man. Bob is of a small stature, but when I hear him
> talk, he talk big. When it comes to the feelings and reac-
> tions I get from Bob, it was always too spiritual to even
> mention or talk about. Even from when he was a small
> child coming up.

In few ways did the boy seem typical. He was
independent, yet rarely disobedient; he knew his
own mind but seldom argued; he was solitary but
made friends easily; he was confident but shy. He
started school at four, a year earlier than normal,
because the teacher said it was obvious that he had
the intelligence of a child twice his age. Later he
would say, "Me not have education; me have inspiration. If I was educated I would be a damn fool."
Yet his teachers remember a student of obvious and
rare ability, who blossomed when he was given
attention: the penetrating stare disguised a gentle
nature that craved love and affection and was perhaps more easily hurt than it wanted to let on. "As
he was shy," recalls one of his teachers, Clarice
Bushey, "if he wasn't certain he was right, he would-
n't always try. In fact, he hated to get answers
wrong, so sometimes you'd really have to draw the
answer out of him. And then give him a clap—he
liked that, the attention." To Bushey, it was obvious
that Nesta received a lot of loving kindness at
home: "I imagined he must have been very much a
mother's pet, because he would only do well if you
gave him large amounts of attention. But it was
obvious he had a lot of potential. When he came by

you to your desk, you knew he just wanted to be touched and held; he was really quite soft. It seemed like a natural thing with him—what he was used to."

In other ways he seemed an ordinary Jamaican child of his time and place. When not in school, he spent his time, as did the other children of Nine Miles, in the fields with his mother and the rest of the large extended Malcolm family, fetching water and performing other chores. Very early in the morning and in the evenings he might be expected to round up and feed the chickens and goats; at any hour he could be seen riding along the steep mountain paths to the fields on his pet donkey, Nimble.

Rural Jamaicans transport a load of fruits and vegetables to a local market. As a boy, Marley would help his family in the fields, growing mangoes, bananas, and other produce.

Most characteristically, he could be found improvising a game of football (soccer). Nesta was crazy about football and would play anywhere, anytime, with anyone; if a ball was not available, an orange peel might do, or a tin can, or a gourd. If playmates were not around, he would play by himself.

There was only one thing Nesta loved more than football: music. It has been said that in Jamaica one can literally breathe in melodies with the sweet tropical air, and little Nesta was truly surrounded by music. One of Omeriah's brothers was an extremely talented instrumentalist who played violin, guitar, and banjo with several of the semiprofessional groups that made dance music at various parish gatherings. Omeriah himself played violin and accordion; even more important, he owned a "sound system"—a turntable, oversize speakers, and an amplifier. Cedella, too, was a musician, a gifted vocalist who sang in the Shiloh Apostolic Church choir and even gave several gospel concerts around St. Ann.

Nesta's mother sang to him constantly, and the boy heard music at home and in the fields, where it made the work go easier, as well as in church and at communal social gatherings. He heard hymns and spirituals; work songs, with their rhythmic calls and responses; popular tunes on his grandfather's sound system; old mournful folk songs, the kind Cedella's own mother used to sing; and the raucous reels and stomps of the homebred Jamaican music known as quadrille, played by the string bands with which his uncle performed. Of all the children in his school, he was the most creative fashioner of his own musical instruments, crafting a guitar out of a sardine box, a piece of wood, and some baling wire and then somehow coaxing melodic sounds from it. "He was very enterprising: you had to commend him on the guitars he made," a teacher remembers. His soft, somewhat high-pitched singing voice made even more of an impression. "During school break," he told an American reporter in 1977, "the teacher, she say, 'Who can talk, talk; who can make anything, make; who can sing, sing'; and me sing." But his musical calling had begun far earlier than that, he explained—had begun, in fact, at the very same moment he entered the world. "How did you start out in singing?" he was asked. "Started out . . . crying," he replied. "Yeah, started out crying, you know?" ❧

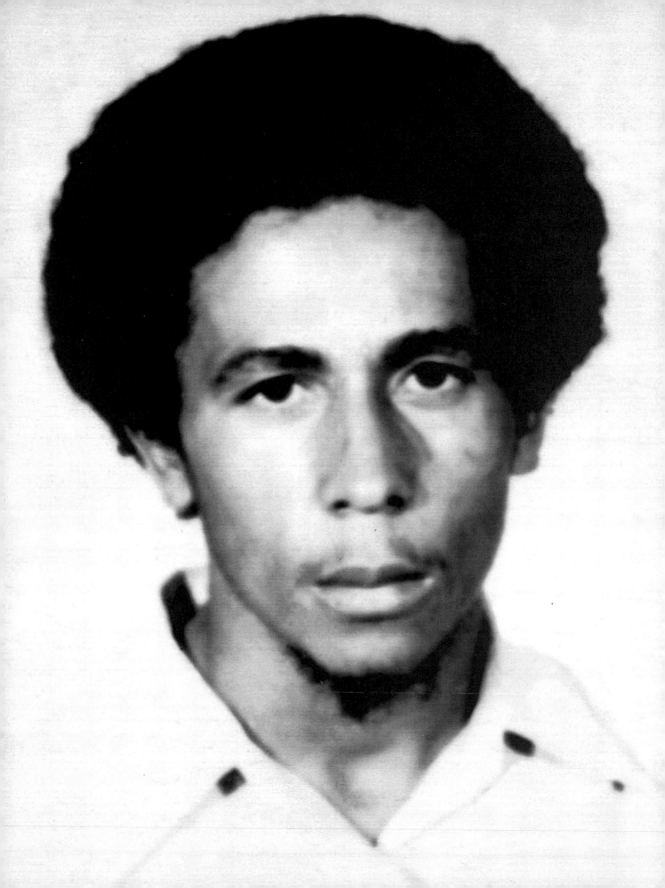

3

TRENCH TOWN ROCK

❧

AT AN IMPRESSIONABLE age, the budding musician was uprooted from the relative comfort of country life. When Nesta was about six years old, his father finally convinced his mother to send him to Kingston, promising the bright young boy access to the city's finer educational system. Reluctantly, after consulting with her father, Cedella agreed, with the understanding that she was not relinquishing custody of her son and could visit him whenever she liked. In Kingston Nesta received a greater education outside the classroom, absorbing lessons about the bleak social conditions plaguing Jamaica's poor that would deeply influence his music and his worldview.

In the 1950s, tens of thousands of black Jamaicans came to Kingston—primarily to the shantytowns that were springing up in the western part of the city—in search of the economic opportunity that was not available to them in the country. With the majority of Jamaica's land held by a tiny white economic elite, most blacks in the countryside lived on and worked relatively small plots of property. Over time the size of those plots was further diminished by inheritance, and the quality of the soil suffered from hard use. Added to these difficulties were the eternal crises that small farmers face—low prices, foreign competition, rising costs of supplies and provisions, and unfavorable weather.

Although never one of Kingston's "rude boys," Marley as a teenager had a tough, pensive quality that earned him the nickname "Tuff Gong."

Year by year, there was less good land for Jamaica's rural population. A survey taken in 1955 revealed that 65 percent of the men and 32 percent of the women in rural Jamaica were unemployed. (While still extraordinarily high at 32 percent, the number for women was lower only because most Jamaican women had domestic responsibilities that kept them from actively seeking outside employment.) Overall, an estimated half of the Jamaican population earned less than $10 a week. For these reasons, an increasingly educated and mobile rural population found itself eager to explore the different experiences and opportunities Kingston had to offer.

But very few of these emigrants found Kingston to be the promised land. More often, it was what its suffering inhabitants dubbed the Trench Town ghetto in West Kingston—the "house of bondage." The sites and names of the various West Kingston shantytowns give some indication of the quality of life there. Trench Town was so called because it sprang up over and around the municipal sewer ditch (or trench) that drained the waste of the older part of the city; the shanties of the Dungle (a Jamaican contraction for Dung Hill) were constructed atop a municipal garbage dump; Back O' Wall spread out behind the wall of the public cemetery.

For obvious reasons, the residents of these benighted areas referred to themselves as "sufferers" or, sometimes, "Israelites" (like the Jews in the Old Testament book of Exodus, they were waiting to be led out of exile in the wilderness). There was no electricity or running water in Trench Town, and the cooling breezes from the mountains never blew down there, leaving it, reputedly, the hottest spot in Jamaica. The residents lived in hovels, shelters, and shanties cobbled together from a fantastic assortment of materials: discarded wood, packing crates, corrugated tin, gasoline cans, newspapers, driftwood gathered from the beaches of Kingston Bay, barrels,

oil drums, fruit crates, and whatever else could be scavenged from the Dungle. Jobs were even harder to come by than they were in the countryside; harder still to maintain, in the eyes of some, was the dignified self-sufficiency of the rural Jamaican. The shacks of Trench Town crowded together one after another; the people cooked outside over open fires in communal yards; they washed outside with water from standpipes or from the sewage ditches, where they relieved themselves as well. Pigs, goats, and chickens roamed free.

The more fortunate residents of Trench Town lived in "government yards"—public housing constructed by the British government after the great hurricane of 1951 blew most of the shanties away. The government yards were simple cement or stucco buildings, a couple of stories tall, usually constructed in a horseshoe shape around a sometimes gated communal yard. Each building might contain

The Chicken Foot Market reflects the poverty endured by residents of West Kingston. "By day, Trench Town looks like an old bombsite of sodden shacks, scorched earth, and improbable tropical scenery," observes Marley biographer Stephen Davis. "By night . . . [it] looks like a desolate war zone of zinc, cement, and scrap."

a dozen or so apartments, each with a couple of rooms. In the more luxurious facilities, two apartments generally shared a kitchen, and several apartments would share whatever indoor sanitary facilities there were. More often, cooking was done outside in the yard, where residents also washed up at a communal standpipe. Marley would memorialize the essentially communal life lived in these government yards in perhaps his most famous song, "No Woman, No Cry."

Norval Marley, being a member of the white ruling class, lived in the better part of Kingston, but that did not make his son's life any easier. As soon as Nesta arrived in the city, his father surrendered him to the custody of a family friend, an old, sickly white woman whom the boy knew only as Mrs. Grey. Nesta stayed with her for about a year, fetching her groceries and coal and running other errands, sporadically attending school, and all the time wondering heartbrokenly why his mother did not come to look for him. Cedella, meanwhile, was frantic with worry; after initially giving her placid assurances about Nesta's well-being, Norval Marley then steadfastly refused to inform her of the boy's whereabouts.

Only the greatest good fortune brought about the reunion of mother and son. While visiting Kingston one day, an acquaintance of Cedella's saw Nesta walking down the Spanish Town Road. "Where is me mother?" the boy immediately asked. "Ask her why she don't come look for me." Surprised by the encounter and unaware of the particulars of Nesta's situation, the woman did not think of asking the boy for his exact address. Nevertheless, Cedella went to the city to look for her son. Her friend had told her that she thought Nesta had mentioned a certain street, so Cedella started her search there. The first person she asked seemed to know about the boy, and then Nesta himself came running around the corner.

He had obviously been well taken care of, for he was heavier and more solid than before. So was she, the youngster mischievously told his mother. He then took her to see Mrs. Grey, who, after learning why Cedella had not come to visit her son sooner, agreed without argument that Nesta should return home with his mother. "He was very handy to Mrs. Grey," Cedella later told Stephen Davis, one of Marley's biographers, "and the two of them helped each other. You could see she was helping him from her heart. But he told us right away he wanted to go home."

Back in St. Ann, Nesta resumed the old routine of school, chores, and football. Those closest to him noticed a change, however; he seemed even more serious than before. He quickly lost the weight he had gained in the city and in fact became dangerously thin, as if something was burning away from within him. When asked, he now refused to read palms, informing those who requested that he had found a new way to prophesy: his talents were now all to be devoted to music. "No," he would say, "I'm not reading no more hand: I'm singing now." With her father's help, Cedella had opened up a little grocery store, and customers there would often pay Nesta to sing for them.

Despite his return to the peaceful countryside, Nesta's life was now somewhat unsettled. Still very young, Cedella was trying to find herself and became increasingly dissatisfied with the quiet life of St. Ann. As she tried various situations in different towns, her son was often entrusted to the care of relatives. Though they were certainly more trustworthy than his father, who died in 1955, Nesta nonetheless missed the company and care of his mother.

Finally, in 1955, Cedella decided to move to Kingston. "Oh, I just had to get out of the country," she told Stephen Davis. "Every young girl in St. Ann want to come out of the country and, you know, shake up themselves a little bit. So I want to go to Kingston and try also." As she initially made her way in the unfamiliar and intimidating world of West Kingston, she stayed with various relatives and tried to find stable work. In a short time she set up house in a one-room apartment with Thaddeus "Taddy" Livingston, a married man (who was not living with his wife) with whom she had become romantically involved back in St. Ann.

By 1957 she succeeded in obtaining one of the coveted apartments in a government yard, at 19 Second Street in Trench Town, and was finally able to send for Bob, as the boy now preferred to be called. Livingston's oldest son, Neville "Bunny" Livingston, who was two years younger than Bob, had become close friends with Bob in St. Ann and joined him in Kingston. The best friends became stepbrothers of a sort: although Cedella Marley and Taddy Livingston never married, they had a daughter, Pearl, in 1962. Together, this makeshift family unit faced the difficult life of Trench Town. Finding the money to pay Bob's private school tuition always presented a challenge, but one Cedella willingly met each term. "I never have to beg nobody or borrow from nobody," she proudly recalled. "I could pay his fee, then save again to buy his shoes. I can't remember a time when I was so badly off that I couldn't find food for him. And he was not a child that demand this or demand that. Never have no problem with him: always obedient, would listen to me. Sometimes he get a little mad with me, but it never last for time."

Always independent, Bob now found excitement in the city streets that kept him away from home. It was a lot easier to round up a group of boys for a football game, for example, and Bob's love of the sport was undiminished. Other activities wor-

ried his mother more, however. In Trench Town, hanging out and boyish mischief all too easily progressed to more serious trouble and even criminal behavior. With their future prospects so seemingly dim, their opportunities for advancement so limited, West Kingston youth were quick to act out their frustration. By the early 1960s the "rude boys" of the West Kingston ghetto had become Jamaica's most troubling social phenomenon. Inspired by American gangster films, martial arts flicks, and the "spaghetti Westerns" of directors such as Sergio Leone, they celebrated criminal behavior, pointless violence, and disrespect toward all established authority as the only means of rebellion available to them. The "rudie's" weapon of choice was the ratchet knife, a kind of curved German-made switchblade, and if the liquor-store holdup or his latest ganja deal netted him enough cash, he preferred to dress in gangster finery—broad-brimmed hats, wide

Marley and his mother shared an apartment in this government yard with Thaddeus Livingston and his son Bunny. Although the building appears run-down, such living quarters were considered highly desirable in the West Kingston ghetto.

ties, and platform shoes. The rudies' greatest hero was Vincent "Ivanhoe" Martin (most often known as Rhyging, which in Jamaican patois means "wild" or "foolhardy"), a gun-toting self-styled ghetto Robin Hood whose killing of three policemen was the ultimate act of defiance in the eyes of the rudies.

While never actually a rude boy himself, Bob came from the same tough environment, and he certainly numbered rudies among his friends. It was next to impossible not to, if one wanted to get by; it was the rare West Kingston family that never had a member in trouble with the law, and Trench Town mothers considered that they had defied the odds if their boys made it to 14—the age in Jamaica at which lower-class youths usually quit school—without landing in jail.

Although no stranger to the roughest aspects of Trench Town life, Bob possessed qualities that seemed to guide him through safely. Very small and generally soft-spoken, he still exuded an aura that deterred people from messing with him. His slightness was combined with a wiry strength, and his skill as a footballer won him much respect; his pensiveness made his few words that much more powerful, and he exhibited a kind of intelligent presence, a charisma, that made others pay attention to him. He seemed always to be watching, thinking about something, waiting for something. Essentially gentle, he could be fierce if the situation required it; when pushed, he pushed back, and he never backed down. On the street they called him the Tuff Gong, and it was said that if you wanted to start something with him, you had better be prepared to finish it, because he would. "You never take popgun to stop alligator," was how the rudies put it. "Same with Bob."

Cedella tried to steer Bob away from the streets, but with little success. Occupied with her own struggle, she did not have as much time to spend with him as she would have liked, and as he grew older, her strong-minded boy became even harder to control. "Bob, these people, these boys who are around you, seem like bad boys," she once warned. "A man is known by the company he keeps."

"Yes, Mama, they *are* bad boys," Bob replied. "But I not going do nothing that is wrong, you know?"

"I *know* you ain't going do nothing that is wrong," Cedella said, "but *these people* can go do bad and because you're in their company, they might lead the police to believe you are in league with them."

"Mama, they don't tell me what to do," Bob insisted. "Nobody can get me into any trouble. My friends, I tell *them* what to do."

As his songs would later demonstrate, Bob fully grasped the despair, the hopelessness, the poverty, and the waste of ghetto life, but he experienced— and expressed—the many other more positive aspects of everyday existence there that the upper-class denizens of Jamaica always overlooked: joy, wisdom, kindness, generosity, dignity, and beauty. "Me grow stubborn you know," Bob later explained of his coming of age in Trench Town. "Me grow without mother or father. Me no have no parent for have no big influence upon me. Me just grow in the ghetto with the youth. Stubborn, no obey no one; but we had qualities, and we were good to one another." ❧

4

CATCH A FIRE

❦

Bunny Livingston, Bob Marley, and Peter Tosh perform as the Wailing Wailers in 1965. "They needed a lot of polishing," remembered producer Clement Dodd, "but Bob had a gift. . . . He had the makings."

THE ONE THING Trench Town was undeniably rich in was music. For the sufferers, music was perhaps the most affordable form of entertainment available, as well as the most accessible means of expression. Bob Marley had sustained his love for music—he made his singing debut in 1959 at a Queens Theatre talent show, where he won a pound (roughly the equivalent of five dollars) and listened to a wide variety of styles. By the late 1950s, even some of the poorest Jamaicans could afford a cheap transistor radio, and at night in the yards, with the wind blowing from the north, American radio stations—from Miami and even New Orleans—came in clear as a bell. Arriving over the airwaves was American rhythm and blues, as performed by such artists as Brook Benton, Ray Charles, Fats Domino, and Ruth Brown. Especially popular with young Jamaicans were the harmonies of male vocal groups such as the Moonglows, the Impressions, and Marley's beloved Drifters. The silky vocals of Nat King Cole and Sam Cooke were favorites, as were the somewhat more exuberant jump blues of Louis Jordan, the flamboyant, pioneering rock and roll of Little Richard, and the relentless funk of James Brown. Even American country music was admired, with Jim Reeves, the East Texas hillbilly with the celebrated "touch of velvet" in his voice, somewhat improbably claiming a wide following among black

45

Jamaicans. The hundreds of thousands of Jamaicans who had to emigrate to the United States to find work were assured the warmest welcome home if they brought with them a batch of the latest records from the American charts.

It was the fiercely competitive proprietors of Kingston's sound systems who most desperately desired such discs. A sound system was a kind of mobile discothèque. It usually consisted of a turntable, microphones, amplifiers, and 30, 40, or even 50 speakers, each of them the size of a large filing cabinet or bureau. Tied together by a rat's nest of cables and wires, these "houses of joy" or "power towers" could then unleash a barrage of sound as the 78s were amped up to the volume of a thunderclap. Trucked from place to place, these systems supplied the residents of West Kingston with up-to-the-minute music. On weekends, the sound-system proprietors would stage "jump-ups," as the huge outdoor dances were called. Hundreds, even thousands, of the sufferers would come together to dance to the booming sounds, socialize with one another, and eat and drink.

The sound-system proprietors and their disc jockeys were the first stars of the fledgling Jamaican music industry. The DJs did much more than cue up records on turntables. They had to work the crowd, understanding its mood and gauging a sequence of songs that would keep everyone in the groove, letting people "simmer down" as their energy began to flag and then raising the temperature to a boil with a new track. Using several turntables at once, the DJ might segue from a popular instrumental section of one hit right into the rhythm groove of another, creating, in a sense, a new track. In between songs, over a repeating instrumental riff maintained by holding the turntable arm in a desired place so that it did not progress across the vinyl, or over a so-called dub track (an instrumental version of a popular song), he would improvise rhymes, often boastful proclamations of his sexual prowess, ribald tales, commentary on current events or happenings in the community, exhortations to the dancers, or putdowns of rival sound-system operators. The sound-system dances were thus one of the many birthplaces of today's rap music.

By the late 1950s, the sound-system proprietors had begun to set up their own recording studios, capitalizing on the rich local talent. Since there was a wealth of exceptional musicians who had little opportunity to record, the operators were able to establish a stranglehold on the Jamaican recording industry, paying new artists cut-rate flat fees for a record without royalties. Among the newest generation of aspiring Jamaican musicians—the youth

The silky harmonies and smooth look of groups like the Drifters inspired the young Marley.

who had been inspired by the new sounds from America and had created the fast-paced hybrid known as ska—the desire to make records, even on such one-sided terms, was fierce.

No one was more driven in this regard than Bob Marley. The multiplicity of influences—musical and otherwise—that he had been exposed to in the city had only intensified his love of music, excited his creativity and imagination, and inflamed his ambition. When he left school at age 14, his mother found him a position as an apprentice welder, despite his desire to devote all his energies to music. After a short time on the job, a tiny steel splinter became embedded in his eye, and the injury settled the issue for good. Cedella later told the writer Malika Lee Whitney, "[At the hospital] him say, 'You no hear me say is nothing else me want to do beside sing?' And I have to say, 'Really, is true.' "

So Bob Marley became a full-time student in the "reggae college," as some would later call the streets of Trench Town. If reggae did not yet exist as a distinct musical form, the seeds of its development were being planted in West Kingston. Among those doing the planting was a singer, regarded as perhaps Jamaica's finest, named Joe Higgs, who lived in a yard right behind the Marleys. Higgs had recorded several hits, but due to the erratic payment practices of the Jamaican recording industry, even the top musicians seldom earned enough to move out of the yards. (Higgs, for example, received a flat fee of $20 for each of the records he made.) In any event, Higgs was a remarkably able teacher, a man genuinely dedicated to imparting his love and knowledge of music to those serious about learning. For no other compensation than the joy of teaching and making music, Higgs took it upon himself to host nightly gatherings of Jamaican singers and musicians and to coach those just starting out.

Marley was among the most talented and serious

beginners, along with his constant companion, Bunny Livingston. The two, who still made music with makeshift guitars fashioned out of a bamboo staff, strands of electrical wire, and a large sardine can, were regular participants in Higgs's sessions, which often lasted all night. Higgs taught the youths not only the principles of harmony, rhythm, and melody but also how to learn from music seemingly far removed from their own. A demanding teacher, Higgs counseled Marley to listen to modern jazz artists such as John Coltrane. At first Marley could not understand jazz, but at Higgs's insistence, he kept on listening. "After a while, I smoke some ganja, some herb, and get to understand it. Me try to get in the mood where the moon is blue and see the feeling expressed. Joe Higgs helped me understand that music. He taught me many things. Him, y'know, is one heavy music man, Joe Higgs."

Under Higgs's tutelage, Marley's musical development was rapid. As much as talent, he had seriousness and ambition in his favor; more than the other youths around, he seemed to know exactly what he wanted to do. Reminiscences of the period, starting with his own, provide a consistent characterization: a single-minded boy sure of his destination, if not always of the exact route to take to reach it. "Then we used to sing in the back of Trench Town," Marley recalled, "and rehearse plenty until the Drifters came upon the scene, and me love group singing so me just say, well, me have for go look a group."

The first member of that group, of course, was Livingston. The two "spars" (close friends) found a third soulmate during the sessions at Higgs's yard. Tall, extroverted, and angry, carrying himself like a rudie, Hubert Winston McIntosh possessed a genuine acoustic guitar and called himself Peter Tosh. Under Higgs's direction, the three began honing their skills. Although in these early days the group would sometimes feature additional members—most importantly Junior Braithwaite and Beverly Kelso—and perform under different names, the Wailers had been born. "The word *wail* means 'to cry' or 'to moan,' " Tosh later explained. "We were living in this so-called ghetto. No one to help the people. We felt we were the only ones who could express their feelings through music, and because of that the people loved it. So we did it."

Long before the Wailers ever played a gig or made a record, Marley was treating their music as a profession. Both Livingston and Tosh were extremely strong-willed individuals, but Marley outdid the

Joe Higgs, a popular singer and a Rasta, greatly influenced the Wailers as a musical and moral guide. Years later, Higgs briefly performed as a Wailer, filling in for Bunny Livingston in several American shows.

two of them in focus. As Joe Higgs recalled, "Bob was the leader of the group. . . . Bob needed to know about everything, but he was quick. It was kind of difficult to get the group to be precise in their sound and put it over in their harmony structure. Just took a couple of years to get that perfect. But person to person, they were each capable of leading at any time because I wanted each person to be a leader in his own right, able to lead anyone, or to be able to wail. That is where the concept came from."

As Higgs indicates, the Wailers formed a special vocal mixture. Each of the three primary members was capable of handling the lead vocals on a particular song, and in harmony their voices blended together with a naturalness that belied their countless hours of training and rehearsal. Tosh's voice was a deep rumbling baritone, Livingston's a virtual falsetto; together the two were often likened to Jerry Butler and Curtis Mayfield of the Impressions. Marley, meanwhile, sang between the two of them, in a somewhat willowy tenor that was remarkably expressive.

He also had the greatest ability as a songwriter. When not rehearsing, he would spend his time alone with his guitar, devising melodies and lyrics. In crowded Trench Town, genuine solitude, of the kind conducive to artistic creativity, was often difficult to come by. As she recalled for Marley's biographers Adrian Boot and Chris Salewicz, Pauline Morrison was among a group of students who at this time met Marley each day as they returned home from school. Every afternoon they would encounter the aspiring musician as he sat under the shade of a huge tree, working out his own songs on his primitive guitar. Although she remembers him as always being very polite and easygoing, she noticed a reserve, a part of himself he only expressed through music. "It was always the man and his guitar," she said. "It was very rare you could just sit with him and be with him. Because he was a very moody person, the way I see him. Him is very moody. If people were sitting together with him, he would suddenly just get up and go somewhere else. Just to be by himself."

No doubt some of the moodiness Morrison observed was loneliness. At about the time he was forming the Wailers, Marley fell in love for the first time, with a girl who was a neighbor in his yard. Their romance was short-lived, however, because the girl's older brother objected to Marley's mixed ancestry and insisted that she break off the relationship. As Cedella recalls, "Her brother say to Bob, 'We don't want no white man in our breed.' . . . Her family kill off the romance. Them style Bob as a white man."

According to his mother, it was not the only time Marley was made to suffer because of his ancestry. He "bore a sacrifice" because of his white paternity, she said, and the frequent insults he endured certainly contributed to the air of sorrow that some saw in him. "Sometimes he'd come across the resistance of being half-caste," she recalled. "There was a problem with his counterparts: having come through this white father caused such difficulties that he'd want to kill himself and think, 'Why am I this person? Why is my father white and not black like everybody else? What did I do wrong?' He was lost in that: not being able to have anyone to say it's not your fault, or that there's nothing wrong in being like you are. But that was the atmosphere he came up in, that Trench Town environment where everybody is rough."

Marley suffered an even greater loss not long thereafter. With the birth of her daughter, Pearl, in 1962, Cedella at last determined for good that there was little future in her relationship with Thaddeus Livingston. She decided, as so many Jamaicans would during the 1960s, to emigrate to the United

States. She planned to make her new home in the small city of Wilmington, Delaware, where some Malcolm relatives were among the Jamaican immigrant community there. She wanted Bob to come with her and even obtained the necessary documents for him.

But Marley wanted to stay. He had his music now, and that was the most important thing to him; he was 18, "mannish," as the Jamaicans say, if not yet fully a man and ready to stand on his own. Promising to join his mother at some unspecified point in the near future, Marley bid her farewell.

He was now homeless, without a job or any

Joe Higgs's backyard served as the campus for Trench Town's "reggae college." Every night young musicians gathered here to study and rehearse under Higgs's patient coaching. Marley later celebrated these times in his classic song "No Woman, No Cry."

source of steady income, but Trench Town youths were used to looking out for one another. One of Marley's closest friends was a young man named Vincent Ford, whom everyone called Tartar. Four years older than Marley, Tartar had gone out on his own a lot younger. While still a teenager, Tartar had earned his living as a chef at a boys' school, but by this time he made money from the little "kitchen" he set up in his yard on First Street. One of many such unlicensed, unofficial establishments in Trench Town, Ford's kitchen, called the "casbah" by his friends, sold the Jamaican equivalent of fast food—calaloo, dumplings, roast yam, and bread-fruit. Much later on in the evenings, the kitchen table would be cleared for some gambling, which typically would go on almost till morning. Then the table would be cleared again, and Marley would finally have a place to sleep.

In the hours after midnight, Marley would sit near the huge bonfire that was always kept burning in Tartar's yard, playing guitar and singing by the dancing firelight. Livingston was usually there with him, and Tosh, and sometimes another friend, Junior Braithwaite, who was a member of the Wailers for a time. A somewhat older man, George Headley Robinson, whom everyone called Georgie, took responsibility for maintaining the fire and tak-ing care of the musicians. A fisherman, he built the fire each night and stoked it with driftwood he picked up while working. The day's catch was offered to feed all the musicians and listeners who gathered there, and Georgie "would sit there shirt-less all night," says Tartar, "tending the flames as they played." When they woke in the morning, Georgie would brew a huge kettle of bush tea and a communal bowl of cinnamon-flavored cornmeal porridge.

No words could capture the sorrowful joy of those times better than Marley's most beloved song,

"No Woman, No Cry," a musical evocation of that period in his own life when the sadness of the have-nots was tempered by hope; when loneliness was alleviated by true friendship uncomplicated by material concerns or the thought of gain; when a mood of despair could be lifted by a simple song; when the struggle was redeemed by a sharing of the burden. "Where the living was hardest," Marley knew, amid the crime, poverty, and desolation, there were also values that were all too often over-looked, truths lost in the pursuit of progress. "Good friends we have, oh good friends we've lost along the way / In this great future you can't forget your past / So dry your tears, I say / And everything's gonna be alright," he would write in "No Woman, No Cry," remaining firmly in touch with the suffer-ers at a time when his own stardom was on the rise. Georgie was mentioned by name in the lyrics, and Marley gave his composer's credit for the song to Tartar, who had by that time become disabled by diabetes. The song held a special place not only in the hearts of Marley's fans but in his own heart as well. "Me really love 'No Woman, No Cry,' " Marley later said, "because it mean so much to me, so much feeling me get from it. Really love it." ☙

5

SIMMER DOWN

❦

FOR THE WAILERS, the joy of making music was often matched and even exceeded by the frustration of doing business in the Jamaican music industry. Marley experienced this aggravation before the Wailers even made their first recordings. In 1961, when he was 16 and just starting to organize the Wailers, Marley convinced Leslie Kong, a Chinese-Jamaican restaurateur who also owned his own record label and store, to let him cut a few sides. Like the sound-system operators, Kong had recognized there was money to be made in recording Jamaican musicians, and in just a couple of years' time he had released numerous hit songs and recorded many important Jamaican singers, including the prolific Derrick Morgan and another singer-songwriter named James Chambers, whom Kong rechristened with the stage name Jimmy Cliff. Cliff's hit "Dearest Beverley" was the first song Kong recorded, and he adopted the name Beverley for his record label.

There are varying versions as to how Marley came to Kong's attention. By all accounts, he used to hang around Beverley's record store, pestering the staff for a chance to sing for the boss but always being rebuffed. At that point, either Jimmy Cliff or Derrick Morgan convinced Kong that he ought to listen to Marley sing. Kong had Marley record a half dozen or so of his songs at Federal Studio.

Singer Jimmy Cliff adopts a defiant stance as a rude boy in the cult film The Harder They Come. *The Wailers gave expression to the rudies' rebellious discontent in such songs as "Simmer Down" and "Rude Boy."*

"Judge Not" was the first to be released, under the name Robert Marley. Although Marley was still many years from embracing Rastafari, the song nonetheless anticipated the moral concerns and biblical tone of his greatest work. "While you talk about me," the song warned, "someone else is judging you." It was followed by "Terror" backed with "One Cup of Coffee," which were released under the name of Bobby Martell, Kong having taken it upon himself—without consulting the artist—to change Marley's name.

None of the songs did particularly well, and Marley was paid only a paltry sum—the equivalent of about $20—for his musical work. He had difficulty collecting even that and quickly broke off the relationship with Kong, feeling exploited. "We will work together again someday," the willful singer predicted to the producer, "and you will make a lot of money off of me, but you will never be able to enjoy it." Kong had a reputation as a tough character who did not scare easily, but Marley's words unnerved him. Kong felt he had been told something that Marley somehow mysteriously knew with a deep inner certainty. It spooked him, and the story made the rounds in Trench Town for a long time.

The discouraging experience with Kong only spurred Marley's determination to make the Wailers a success. Marley played a handful of solo shows—some observers, such as Derrick Morgan, thought that at this early point in his career he was a better dancer than singer—but he devoted most of his energies to his endless rehearsal sessions with Joe Higgs and the Wailers. For nearly two years the group's only reward for their hard work was the certainty that they were getting better. But for Marley, the hard times were getting even harder. Tartar's boundless hospitality left his kitchen often too crowded for Marley to stay there, and the singer spent a six-month period living on the streets, sneaking at night onto rooftops to sleep, sometimes staying for a day or two at one of the small Rasta colonies out on the beaches.

Finally, in late December 1963, Alvin Patterson brought the Wailers to audition for Clement Dodd at Dodd's Studio One in the northernmost part of Trench Town. Patterson, whom the Wailers called Franceesco or just Seeco, was recognized as one of the island's master musicians. A constant participant in the sessions at Higgs's yard and a great booster of the Wailers', Patterson was a virtuoso in the traditional Jamaican folk music of *burru* drumming, which utilizes three drums. Derived from African tradition, burru drumming had been used in the Jamaican countryside to welcome home liberated prisoners, and modern practitioners such as Patterson sought ways to incorporate elements of burru into Jamaican popular music. Burru drumming was also featured at the periodic Rasta gatherings known as *Nyabinghis*, which the historian Leonard Barrett defines as "a gathering of the brethren for inspiration, exhortation, feasting, smoking, and social contact."

Clement "Sir Coxsone" Dodd, meanwhile, was perhaps the single most important figure in the Jamaican music industry. A pioneering sound-system operator, one of the first to make great use of American records, Dodd was also one of the first to branch out into music production on his own. Noted for his idiosyncracies—he addressed all males as "Jackson," for example—Dodd was as talented as he was eccentric. Though not a musician himself, Dodd was blessed, said the great Jamaican guitarist Ernest Ranglin, with "an extraordinary pair of ears" and an ability to communicate musical ideas in language that musicians could translate into new sounds. "He was really the man," said Ranglin, "the man who came up with the ideas. But he couldn't play, so he would come and explain it to us. After

Though not a musician himself, Clement "Sir Coxsone" Dodd pioneered the development of the Jamaican music industry, inspiring the creation of ska and recording such authentic Jamaican artists as the Skatalites and the Wailers.

explaining it, I always knew what the man wanted."

The "us" Ranglin referred to was the superb house band Dodd assembled at Studio One, consisting, among others, of Ranglin and Jah Jerry on guitars; trombonist Don Drummond (whom the masterful American jazz pianist George Shearing classified as one of the top jazz musicians in the world); saxophonists Rolando Alphonso, Tommy McCook, and Lester Sterling; Johnny "Dizzy" Moore on trumpet; Lloyd Nibbs on drums; Lloyd Brevitt and Cluett Johnson on bass; and Jackie Mittoo on keyboards. The group became known as the Skatalites. Having tired of the American sounds that many Jamaican artists persisted in slavishly imitating, Dodd was looking for something more homegrown.

"I need something to get away from these blues," Sir Coxsone put it to Ranglin one day. What Ranglin and his musical colleagues came up with was ska, an extremely fast-paced rhythmic sound, accentuated with jazzlike horns and with the emphasis on the off beat, that combined the best features of contemporary Jamaican and American music, particularly in its intensity and intricate vocal harmonies. Various explanations are offered for the derivation of the name given the music. Ranglin says ska was essentially a nonsense word coined by musicians "to talk about the *skat! skat! skat!* scratchin' guitar strum that goes behind the rest of the music." Others say the name came from "skavoovee," a slang term of approval popular in Jamaica at the time that was often used by bassist Cluett "Clue-J" Johnson, who helped Ranglin create the sound. Similarly, the peculiar, entrancing qualities of the music were said to be the result of the musicians' attempt to emulate the way the nighttime music from the States faded in and out on the cheap transistor radios in the West Kingston yards. Ranglin provided another source of origin as well: "We just wanted it to sound like the theme music from one of those westerns that were on TV all the time in the late 1950s."

Ska was the sound dominating Marley's first recordings for Leslie Kong and for most of the records the Wailers would make for Clement Dodd at Studio One. The group auditioned for Sir Coxsone beneath the mango tree in the dusty yard behind the studio, where on many days to come they would while away the minutes between takes in the rusted-out shell of an old van, smoking the occasional spliff and practicing their harmonies. Impressed by their vocal sophistication and evident seriousness, Dodd was even more taken by the original material they sang for him, especially "Simmer Down," a song that addressed the escalating violence of the rude boys. Still searching, as always, for authentic Jamaican music, Dodd recognized that "Simmer Down" and the Wailers were exactly what he had been looking for. With their eternal screwfaces—"We were frowny, frowny people," Peter Tosh conceded about that time—and rude-boy aura, the group already had the necessary "street" credibility. And as one of the first Jamaican songs to directly capture the situation in the Kingston ghetto in the language—musically and lyrically—of the ghetto dwellers themselves, "Simmer Down" was the perfect vehicle with which to introduce the group to the public.

Recorded in late 1963, with a sizzling instrumental track provided by the Skatalites that featured blistering solos by Ranglin and Alphonso, "Simmer Down" reached the top of the Jamaican charts in February 1964 and spent several months blaring from seemingly every West Kingston barroom jukebox. Though the song urged the rude boys to temper their violent ways, it also clearly implied that the Wailers understood their anger and frustration and were, in fact, on their side. "Simmer down," the Wailers sang, their own voices seething, "the battle will get hotter." Hold your anger, that is, until the time is right. The music was pure, relentless ska, the rude boys' own hopped-up rhythm of choice, clearly identifying the Wailers, in the popular mind, as incipient street rebels. As the Trench Town denizens immediately realized, this was music made by the have-nots for the have-nots.

That image was solidified by the various hits the Wailers recorded with the Skatalites for Sir Coxsone over the next several years, including "Rude Boy," "Rule Dem Rudie," "Steppin' Razor," and "Jailhouse." During that time, the group also became almost as well known for its love songs, such as "I Need You" and Marley's achingly beautiful "It Hurts To Be Alone," which displayed the soft side that those who got beyond the screwface always found so endearing.

In addition, the band covered American songs, such as Marley's rewrite of his beloved Drifters' "On Broadway" and the group's version of Aaron Neville's "Ten Commandments of Love," not to mention more unlikely remakes, such as Burt Bacharach's "What's New, Pussycat?" and Irving Berlin's "White Christmas." If such songs seemed odd material for the rebellious Wailers, as incongruous as the gold lamé suits with which Dodd outfitted them for their numerous appearances around the island, the Wailers themselves were not greatly bothered by any possible contradiction. "Knowing that we found reality and righteousness, we relaxed," said Tosh. "So when you saw us in the slick suits and things, we were just in the thing that was looked on as the thing at the time. So we just adjusted ourselves materially."

Gold lamé could not hide the group's originality. "They have a different sense of music," explained Alton Ellis, whose own recordings often competed with the Wailers' on the Jamaican charts, "and we all love it. . . . Bob's sound was always different: it mesmerised me from those times. His music always have a roots sense of direction. Not even just the words—I'm talking about the melody that him sing, the feel of the rhythm. Always a bit different." Onstage, said Ellis, Marley was a "ragamuffin." Other Jamaican acts sought to emulate the sophistication and polish of the American vocal groups, but "him [Marley] was a rebel: jump up and throw himself about onstage. The Wailers them just mad and free: just threw themselves in and out of the music, carefree and careless."

Paradoxically, the spontaneity and rebelliousness that Ellis and others responded to in the Wailers' music was made possible only by intense preparation and endless rehearsal: their complete mastery of the material allowed the Wailers to express it with perfect freedom. That dedication, in turn, was made possible by a mutual friendship as tight as the group's harmonies. As Johnny Moore of the Skatalites observed, "At the time they were very young and vibrant and you could see they were very good friends: they were very, very close to one another. They really did care about each other. I guess that's why they made a success of it as it was."

For all the musical benefits of the Wailers' association with Dodd, the relationship was destined to be short-lived. After their initial audition, Dodd had signed them on his usual terms—a flat fee of 15 pounds (about $60) per record, with no royalties. As newcomers to the recording game, with no clout in the industry, the Wailers had no choice but to agree. Dodd's subsequent decision to put the group on a weekly salary of three pounds did little to ease their discontent; for that money, they found, they were expected to be on almost permanent call at Studio One, available around the clock to record backing vocals on other tracks Dodd was producing, or to coach, rehearse, and prepare other groups. If their inquiries about royalties or more equitable arrangements grew too strident, Dodd referred them to the pistol he kept in his studio as the ultimate answer to such ingratitude.

Of the three Wailers, Marley was perhaps the most distressed by the group's relationship with Dodd. The producer liked to tell people that he had "adopted" the Wailers, and he had, in fact, given Marley a home of sorts, a spare room in a shack behind the studio where the musician slept on an unhinged wooden door laid on two cinder blocks. The musical education he was receiving at Studio One was priceless too; constant proximity to Ernest Ranglin had improved Marley's guitar playing immeasurably, and he was being exposed to all kinds of intriguing new sounds—especially those of the Beatles and Bob Dylan, whose classic "Like a Rolling Stone" Marley would rework for the Wailers—that were expanding his own musical creativity. Yet there was certainly something wrong when the leader of the hottest group in Jamaican music—at one point in 1965, records by the Wailers occupied positions one, two, three, seven, and nine on the Jamaican charts—was living penniless in a donated shack.

Complicating the situation by the end of 1965 was Marley's relationship with Alvarita Anderson, an aspiring nurse and teacher who also taught Sunday school and sang with her own Motown-inspired group, the Soulettes. The dirt path the Wailers walked each day to Studio One wound right behind the house where Anderson lived with her aunt, and like others in Trench Town she was fascinated by these boys who "sounded like angels" but looked to her, as she watched them pass by every day, "like rough little guys." (At six feet, Tosh was by far the tallest of the Wailers; Marley was, at most, five foot eight, and Livingston was several inches shorter than that.) Anderson, known to everyone as

Rita, was too shy to introduce herself, but in time a friend arranged for the Soulettes to audition for Dodd, and she reminded the Wailers, who were present at the time, that she was the girl they saw each day as they went to work.

Impressed by the Soulettes, Dodd agreed to record them, and he assigned Marley to be their "manager"—that is, to rehearse them and prepare them for their professional debut. It was not a decision that made Anderson especially happy, as she later recalled:

> Bob was very strange from them times. He didn't talk much, and he didn't laugh much. He was more *observing*. Also, he would lead the rehearsals, and we were very scared of him because of the discipline he would put on his rehearsals and the type of harmony that we sing. So he wasn't a favorite of ours at that time. We used to think that this man is *very* cross. Nothing but music. No girls, no anything. He was totally different. . . . He was very firm about what we were about: if you come to the studio, you don't come to play; you're here to work. As long as Marley was there, that discipline was established.

Marley, Livingston, and Tosh show off their gold lamé outfits to Beverly Kelso, who occasionally performed with them. Skatalite Johnny Moore remembered that the Wailers were just beginning to create their own style: "From that time they realized that trying to be the Impressions was not what they should be doing, they really checked into themselves and got into it. You can hear it in the music."

She was thus stunned when, after several weeks, Livingston informed her that Marley was in love with her. Even with his secret revealed, Marley found it hard to speak of his feelings directly; he preferred to write love letters, which Livingston would deliver. Initially attracted to Tosh, who possessed a personality that could be as outgoing and charming as it was sometimes menacing, Anderson now began to look at Marley differently. "You have to be prepared to meet him," she explained. "Then when you do, you find that behind all of that he is the nicest person, like an angel."

His developing relationship with Anderson gave Marley one more reason for wanting a more settled

Marley and Rita Anderson share a happy moment at their wedding on February 10, 1966. However, Marley left his bride the next day—just as his own father had done—to make his fortune in America.

existence. Even before the two had become a couple, he was growing desperate to escape the barren quarters Dodd had given him. His seriousness and air of withdrawal had more to do with just temperament, Anderson learned; he was literally haunted. One day, he confided to her that he got almost no sleep at night and felt his strength being gradually drained from his body: a duppy had been set upon him and did its evil work each night in the shack behind Studio One. Anderson was extremely skeptical, but when she spent one night with Marley in the room she was awakened from sleep by a terrifying sensation that "felt as though someone came into the room and held me down. You'd try to get out of this grip and feel as though you were going into a trance; you couldn't speak; you couldn't talk; you couldn't see anything—you just felt the sensation." Frightened into belief, she brought Marley home to the house where she lived with her aunt, who, when she realized how serious the couple were about their relationship, agreed to build a little shack for them to live in.

A short time later, on February 10, 1966, Bob Marley and Rita Anderson were formally married. The ceremony did not mean that their life together was settled in any meaningful way, however, for on the very next day Bob left—alone—for America. Discouraged by the Jamaican music business, he knew he had to find another way, and he hoped to find some answers in the States. ☙

6

RASTA, ROOTS, AND REGGAE

❦

WHILE RITA MARLEY was pining away for her husband—"Is this what they call marriage?" she often asked Tartar, who looked after her in his friend's absence—Bob was thinking things out in Wilmington, Delaware, where he was reunited with his mother. There, he held a succession of odd jobs—working as a laboratory assistant, washing dishes in a restaurant, driving a forklift in a factory, and manning the assembly line in a Chrysler automobile plant—while laying his plans. Musical success had not translated into financial reward for the Wailers; if the group was to control its own destiny, it needed financial as well as artistic independence. Accordingly, Marley planned to use the money he made in the United States—a large sum by Jamaican standards—to start his own record label, enabling the Wailers to break free of Dodd.

Marley returned to Kingston in October 1966, bringing with him $700 for the start of the record company and the first electric guitar he had ever owned. His return came at a time when dramatic changes were occurring that would affect the Wailers and their music. During the short time that he had been gone, a monumental event had occurred: in April 1966, Emperor Haile Selassie of

In the late 1960s, Earl "Wire" Lindo, Aston "Family Man" Barrett, Marley, Peter Tosh, Carlton Barrett, and Bunny Livingston (left to right) combined to help create Jamaica's newest sound, reggae.

Ethiopia had visited Jamaica.

For the island's Rastas, Selassie's arrival represented much more than the stopover of a foreign dignitary on a state visit. It was nothing less than the incarnation of the Messiah on Jamaican soil. For the ever-growing number of Rastas, Selassie's crowning as emperor of Ethiopia in 1930 had fulfilled biblical prophecy, most notably as expressed in the fifth chapter of Revelations, which discusses "the Lion of the tribe of Judah." Followers also cited Marcus Garvey's call to "look to Africa for the crowning of a Black King; he shall be the Redeemer." (Some students of Garvey and Rastafari now argue that it was actually one of his followers who uttered this famous remark, not Garvey himself.)

Selassie's ascendancy was regarded by many black Jamaicans as the realization of religious prophecy. His given name, Ras Tafari Makonnen, was adopted as the name—Rastafari—by which the new religion became known. That religion, which held Selassie's divinity as a central tenet, drew on a long tradition of Ethiopianism among Jamaica's blacks, in which Africa, Ethiopia in particular, was viewed as the lost homeland and promised holy land of an exiled people—beliefs that held obvious appeal for a people acutely aware of their slave heritage. Rastas believe their religion to be the pure and uncorrupted culmination of Judeo-Christian traditions, as maintained over the years in the Ethiopian Orthodox Church. Selassie (the name means "Power of the Holy Trinity") is considered the 225th king in a direct line of descent from the biblical King Solomon and the Queen of Sheba.

For Rastas, the Bible is a sacred book, and most of them are on familiar, even intimate terms with it. As any Rasta knows, it takes three and a half years, at the rate of a single chapter each day, to read the Bible through from Genesis to Revelation, and few of the genuine believers have not completed this task. They apply their own interpretation to its words, however, and regard the existing Christian churches as corrupt agents of a social system that operates to oppress blacks. Rastas metaphorically liken their situation in Jamaica to the captivity of the Old Testament Jews in Babylon. (In the Bible's New Testament, Babylon is also the name of the great earthly city in the Book of Revelation that is made "desolate" for its sinfulness.) Jamaica is thus literally regarded as hell on earth; Ethiopia is the lost promised land to which the faithful aspire to be ultimately returned; and Zion (a Biblical name for the kingdom of Israel) is the eternal land of redemption and rest awaiting the faithful at the end of one's temporal life on earth. Babylon, for the Rasta, is this temporal existence, in all its entirety and individual facets, as well as all those workings and manifestations of society that keep "I and I" (as the Rasta refers to himself and the rest of the brethren) "downpressed."

Rastas seek as little contact with the system, with Babylon, as possible. Many refuse to vote, pay taxes, send their children to school, or otherwise engage with society. In the early days of the movement, from the 1930s through the 1950s, as it gained adherents among the impoverished elements of Jamaican society, Rastas lived close to nature in encampments in the hills of eastern Jamaica or on the less-frequented beaches, making a subsistence living as small farmers, artists and craftsmen, or fishermen.

Strictly adhering to a diet they consider *ital*— pure, unprocessed, clean— they eat mostly grains, fruits, vegetables, and fish and forbid the consumption of meat and shellfish; beverages likewise are restricted to products that come directly from the earth: water, juices, and herbal teas but not milk or coffee. Rastas disdain the use of most seasonings, such as salt, and prohibit tobacco and alcohol use, which they see as a destructive force that has been pushed on blacks by whites. "Rum mosh up your insides," explained Marley, "Just kill ya, like the system."

Biblical precepts are also the basis for the two best-known Rastafarian identifying characteristics: dreadlocks and ganja use. For scriptural authority on dreadlocks, Rastas cite Leviticus 21:5: "They shall not make baldness upon their head, neither shall they shave off the corner of their beard, nor make any cuttings in their flesh." Accordingly, the Rastaman lets his hair grow out in long, luxurious locks, which, among the most devout, are never cut, combed, or otherwise treated and are washed only with water and natural herbal substances, not soap or chemically manufactured shampoos.

The symbolism of the locks, which operates on many different levels, is extremely important. Most simply, in Jamaica, as in many other countries, long

A Jamaican Rasta prepares food at his commune in the 1970s. Rastas cultivate a righteous, natural way of life by eating unprocessed food, wearing their hair in dreadlocks, and making a subsistence living as farmers, fishermen, or craftsmen.

hair on men often indicates nonconformity or rebellion. Besides representing a natural state, dreadlocks embody a pride in the Rastas' African origin, heritage, and features, expressing a reaction to a convention of upper-class white Jamaican society that equates beauty and all things desirable with whiteness. Though not all Rastas wear the locks, most take pride in their leonine hair as the visible symbol of their faith and rebellion, dubbing their hair "dreadlocks" because of the fear—the dread—it and their person seem to induce in the nonbrethren.

Nothing makes Rastas more dread in the eyes of Jamaican society than their cultivation, sale, and use of ganja. For the Rasta, however, "wisdomweed" is a divine gift, a natural instrument of meditation given by Jah to his people. They find numerous biblical passages that sanction its use, such as Psalms 104:14: "He causeth the grass to grow for the cattle, and herb for the service of man, that he may bring forth food out of the earth." Accordingly, the "holy herb" is used, often communally, as a sacrament, either in large spliffs or in chillums or chalices (pipes).

The opposition of the authorities and the disdain of most elements of Jamaican society did not slow the growth of Rastafari. When Haile Selassie's plane touched down in Kingston on April 21, 1966, more than 100,000 of the brethren awaited him on the tarmac. The size and intensity of the gathering startled the emperor no less than it did the Jamaican government authorities; initially, an overwhelmed Selassie could not be persuaded to leave his jet, and when he emerged he wept. The reception accorded the emperor also alerted the government that this grassroots, hill-country religion was not, as they had long hoped, dying out. The government soon mounted one of its periodic crackdowns on the Rastas, culminating in the bulldozing of Back O' the Wall, with its many Rasta enclaves, in the summer

In 1930, Haile Selassie was crowned emperor of Ethiopia. In the eyes of his followers, the event fulfilled a biblical prophecy; though official records indicate that Haile Selassie died in 1975, he is still revered as the messiah by the large Rastafarian community.

of 1966. The destruction only confirmed what the Rastas believed about the nature of Babylon.

Despite Rita Marley's upbringing in the church, she had come to mistrust the common characterization of the Rastas as dangerous and violent; she was moved by their poverty, their dignity, their humbleness, and the simple beauty of their call for "One Love" to unite all people. On April 21, she was among the huge throng of Jamaicans—even more than gathered at the airport—that lined the streets of Kingston as Haile Selassie's motorcade passed through. Situated with a clear view of the emperor's limousine, she cautiously told herself that she would await a sign of his divinity. As she caught her first glimpse of the Ethiopian ruler, she was disappointed: he was small and slight, not very impressive. But then he looked directly at Rita and waved, revealing the stigmata—the wounds of the crucified Christ in the palm of his hands. Her conversion to the Rastafarian lifestyle was virtually immediate, and she wrote to her husband about the incredibly moving experience.

More than any single event, his embrace of Rastafari brought about the full flowering of Marley's artistry, helping him order his understanding of his individual identity, the nature of Jamaican society, and indeed the very meaning of earthly existence. Paradoxically, that very personal vision would give rise to an art so powerful in its truth and beauty that it transcended the very specific conditions and circumstances involved in its creation to deliver a message of nearly universal impact.

The other Wailers were equally drawn to Rastafari, and the three friends began growing their hair out and living according to Rasta tenets. Using the money Marley had earned in Delaware, they established the Wail 'N' Soul 'M record label (later just Wail 'N' Soul or sometimes Wailing Souls), named in honor of its two acts, the Wailers and

Soulettes. Ska was no longer the sound of Jamaica; the new music was rock steady, a slower, less frantic rhythm with a more pronounced bass line that suited the Wailers just fine. Though they recorded some first-rate sides for Wail 'N' Soul—"Nice Time," "Thank You Lord," "Hypocrites," and "Pyaka," for example—having their own record label proved no guarantee of financial success. Rita and Bob opened a second record store, the Soul Shack, but the business of distributing the records—Rita, mostly, but sometimes Bob, carried them around town to the stores, radio stations, and bars by bicycle—proved exhausting, and the label seldom had enough cash on hand to press enough records to keep up with demand. As a result, the group's popularity once again far exceeded its earnings, even as the increased political and social directness of their songs' lyrics was finding an extremely receptive audience among the sufferers.

Discouraged, for a time the Marleys even left Kingston to try their hands at farming the land Bob's grandfather, Omeriah Malcolm, had left him in Nine Miles. Though the country life was a difficult one, it put him in touch with his roots. "It was different," said Rita, who had spent her entire life in Kingston. "I had to carry water, collect wood to make the fire, and I had to sleep on a little, small bed on the dirt because they didn't have flooring. But it was all out of love—I had decided to do so, and it didn't matter. I was going into the faith of Rastafari and I was seeking to find an independent sort of self. Because Bob was already exposed to this lifestyle, it was a thrill for him to see me just living it. It was something he had decided he would do eventually—just be a farmer and stay in the country and live. So this was always his feeling: his need to go back into the open country, and just be himself."

This more natural way of life reinforced Marley's newfound faith, and it opened a wellspring of creativity in him. Many of the songs he would record in the next few years—some of his most powerful and well-known work, such as "Stir It Up" and "Trench Town Rock"—had their genesis during this retreat to the St. Ann countryside. Before their full return to Kingston in 1970, Bob and Rita were blessed with the birth of two children, daughter Cedella and son David (known as Ziggy), and Bob adopted Rita's child, Sharon, from a previous relationship.

The music business remained a struggle, though. At different times both Livingston and Tosh were arrested for ganja possession and had to serve fairly lengthy sentences, preventing the group from working together. Wail 'N' Soul went bust, forcing the Wailers to hustle up new arrangements. They made a deal with Johnny Nash, a moderately successful black American singer who had become fascinated by Jamaican music and was introduced to Marley at a Rasta gathering where the singer played one extraordinary song after another on his acoustic guitar. Nash and his manager, Danny Sims, immediately arranged to sign Marley to their own publishing company as a songwriter and to place the Wailers on retainer to make demo records for them. The arrangement provided the Wailers with some badly needed income, but it did little to further their career and somewhat shackled them creatively.

Desperate, the group even turned to Marley's old nemesis, Leslie Kong. To that point, the only full-length albums released in Jamaica were simply collections of singles. As a "pep talk" to themselves, the Wailers had composed and recorded a cycle of new songs that were related thematically and reflected their religious and political concerns. They wanted Kong to release the material as a true album, just as other important contemporary performers, most notably the Beatles and Bob Dylan, did with their own music. To their extreme anger, Kong dis-

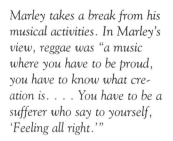

Marley takes a break from his musical activities. In Marley's view, reggae was "a music where you have to be proud, you have to know what creation is. . . . You have to be a sufferer who say to yourself, 'Feeling all right.'"

missed their concerns and insisted on releasing the work as *The Best of the Wailers.* An angry Bunny Livingston echoed Marley's earlier prediction to the producer: "How can you know the best of someone's work," he demanded of Kong, "when we have such a long trod ahead of us? If this is our best to you, it must mean that you are at the end of your life." Kong released the album as he had planned. Less than a week later he dropped dead of a heart attack, at the age of 38, and Livingston's statement, as well as Marley's earlier prediction, was frequently recalled.

Marley foresaw an early death for himself as well, offering a possible explanation for the almost frightening sense of urgency he brought to his music and career. In mid-1969 he was in Wilmington, having returned there to earn some badly needed money on the assembly line at Chrysler, and often thought wistfully of Jamaica and the Wailers. One day a friend sought to console him, assuring him that he had a long life ahead of him in which to produce music. "No, mon," Marley told him quite seriously, "me know I going to die when 36."

He was back in Kingston by the end of the year. A musician who worked with the Wailers around that time remembered the mood being constantly somber, urgent, "always screwface," as he put it. The dread aspect the Wailers were taking on as a result of their embrace of Rastafari and incidents such as the one with Kong did little to ease their way in the music business. Producers preferred to work with musicians who asked fewer questions and were less likely to stand up for their rights.

Lee Perry, however, was not afraid of the Wailers. Fittingly known as the Upsetter or Scratch—"my name is Scratch, from the beginning, and everybody have to start from scratch," Perry explained; "anyone deny that, him fall"—the diminutive, talkative producer was carving out a reputation for himself as one of Jamaica's greatest musical artists. Most importantly, he was being credited with almost single-handedly inventing Jamaica's new sound, a mystifyingly hypnotic music called reggae, which featured a beat even slower than rock steady, one that made you feel, said Scratch, "like you stepping in glue." Though the origin of the word is unknown, its practitioners were sure of its meaning. "Reggae means coming from the people, you know?" explained lead singer Toots Hibbert of Toots and the Maytals, one of the few Jamaican groups that can rightfully consider themselves the Wailers' peers. "Reggae mean *regular* people who are suffering, and don't have what they want."

Perry's collaboration with the Wailers seemed natural. Like them, he had served his time—as a DJ and producer—with Clement Dodd and had left feeling criminally underpaid. Determined, he said, "to upset" the Jamaican music scene with his new sound, he had in his employ the island's foremost instrumental group since the demise of the original Skatalites in 1965. Membership in the Hippy Boys or Upsetters, as the band variously billed itself, alternated around the group's two founders and rhythm section, bassist Aston "Family Man" Barrett and, on drums, Aston's younger brother, Carlton Barrett. Both as fellow Rastas and musicians, the Barretts had long wanted to hook up with the Wailers. "We have a special respect and love for the Wailers, and the whole concept of them," Family Man said. "It was good energy coming from the beginning. . . . The Wailers was the best vocal group, and I group was the best little backing band at the time, so we say why don't we just come together and smash the world?"

With Barrett's band, the Wailers worked with Perry through late 1969 and most of 1970. It was a nearly perfect artistic collaboration. With its simmering, percolating beats, reggae is above all bass-driven music, and in Family Man the Wailers had one of the very best guitarists in the world (as attested to by no less a musical authority than Miles Davis, the peerless American jazz trumpeter), an unusually melodic player who was also a thunderous rhythmic force. "Carly" Barrett was almost as inspired a player, and despite personal differences Perry and Marley immediately established an artistic relationship so close that it was difficult to see, musically, where one left off and the other began.

Counting on Barrett to oversee the instrumentals, Marley began referring to Family Man as his "melodic superintendent," and with his instrumental support the Wailers took on the sound for which they are best known. Without ska's frantic pace, horns, and instrumentation, there was much more space in this music, more even than rock steady had allowed him. The Wailers' vocal harmonies became less studied, rougher, more natural, less consciously imitative of American vocal groups. For Marley, the music was endlessly open, receptive to all kinds of influence and experimentation, including American-style rhythm and blues and doo-wop, church-style backing vocals, tinges of rock guitar, burru drumming, even modern jazz. This openness allowed him to combine his talent for buoyant, infectious melodies with lyrics that displayed a genuine gift for simple yet poetic language, mixing Rastafarian, biblical, and folk wisdom with homespun metaphors, close, distilled observation, and ever-more-direct social and political criticism. Never again would music so outspoken sound so joyful.

Though less widely distributed than his later recordings, and thus less well known, the early recordings Marley and the Wailers made with Perry are regarded by many devotees as their best. Many would become staples of Marley and the Wailers' song catalog and live performances: "Small Axe," "Duppy Conqueror," "Lively Up Yourself," "Kaya," and Tosh's "400 Years." In them, Marley proudly proclaimed that a new day had come; armed with the power of Rastafari, the sufferers could be made free. Jail could not hold them, as he explained in "Duppy Conqueror," nor even the power of the dead: "The bars could not hold me / Force could not control me / They try to keep me down / But Jah put I around . . . I'm a duppy conqueror."

But there were still some things the Wailers could not overcome. Perry packaged the sides the group had recorded for him as three albums—*Soul Rebels*, *Soul Revolution* (sold in some markets as *Rasta Revolution*), and *African Herbsman*—that he sold for distribution in Great Britain and the United States, where large Jamaican immigrant communities created a market. Unfortunately, as Bunny Livingston explained, "We have never made one dime from any of them. Perry refused to give us our money when it came time for us to collect. He said he had decided to just give us some royalties. But we have never seen anything at all. Nothing. Not one penny." When Perry behaved similarly regarding royalties from Jamaican sales of the records, particularly "Duppy Conqueror," Marley, Livingston, and Tosh, with little other recourse, beat him up. A fellow musician teased them, implying that the crazy dreads had only gotten what they deserved: "Hey, only a Rastaman dare sing about duppy." Though Marley would work with Perry again on occasion, the partnership was broken. ❧

7

SONGS OF FREEDOM

❦

ON THE BRINK of greater stardom, the Wailers again turned to the alternative of establishing their own label. Their production company, Tuff Gong, was split in an almost equal three-way partnership between the trio of original Wailers, with Marley holding the slight majority share. Besides funding the start-up cost of the new venture, Marley's close friend Alan "Skill" Cole, Jamaica's greatest soccer star, stayed on with the Wailers in an unofficial yet most important capacity. Counteracting the longtime payoff arrangements between the larger labels and the handful of Jamaican radio stations, Cole applied the necessary muscle to get air time for the Wailers: "We have to go up there and have to beat boy. We go and fight a system where they just have money power. We are on the street; we are street boy. We beat program director, disc jockey. . . . Conk them up in them head and kick them batty. They was fighting us because we was Rastas. Bob Marley was the singer; he was a quiet little brethren. Can't do nothing more than be quiet and give you the best lyrics and the best music. So me just deal with things the right and proper way."

Cole's muscle was not necessary to help the first release on Tuff Gong in 1971, however. "One good thing about music: when it hits you feel no pain," Marley wrote and sang on "Trench Town Rock,"

A passionate, soulful peformer, Marley was regularly observed by his backup singers, the I-Threes, "dancing in the spirit" during performances.

and the sufferers clearly agreed with him. The song topped the Jamaican charts for five months. For Bunny Livingston, "Trench Town Rock" represented the Wailers' true breakthrough, "the tune that made us *really* start to search." "We were now gone into a twelfth dimension," Peter Tosh confirmed.

As the Wailers were catching fire in Jamaica, reggae was breaking through on the international scene. Johnny Nash's reggae-tinged blockbuster album *I Can See Clearly Now*, featuring four Marley songs, went to number one on charts around the world, including the United States. Barbra Streisand was among the many singers who covered at least one of the Marley compositions—in this case, "Guava Jelly"—from the album. In the wake of its success, Nash's manager, Danny Sims, arranged for Marley to go to Stockholm, Sweden, to work on songs for the soundtrack of a proposed film starring Nash.

A short time later, a low-budget movie filmed in Kingston, starring Jimmy Cliff as a talented young musician driven by ghetto life and the greed of the music industry to become a Rhyging-like outlaw, was released in the United States. *The Harder They Come* became one of the longest-running and highest-grossing "cult films" in U.S. history. Its epic reggae soundtrack, featuring tunes by a number of the Wailers' contemporaries, did equally well. Whereas Nash's versions were watered-down, homogenized reggae suited for American pop radio and devoid of political content, *The Harder They Come* was the real thing. Reggae was no longer Jamaica's secret, and Kingston was on its way to becoming the "Third World Nashville." Among white rock musicians, such as Eric Clapton and the Rolling Stones, reggae was soon to become the hippest new sound.

Only one step remained to complete this transformation. From Stockholm, where the cold Scandinavian weather made for an unpleasant stay,

Marley was sent by Sims to London, England. The movie had fallen through, but he was to be joined there by the other Wailers, for the intended purpose of backing Nash on a concert tour. As with many of Sims's ventures, however, this too fell apart, and after just one gig the Wailers found themselves stranded in cold, rainy England, without enough money for return tickets home. To make matters worse, the group got busted for a package of ganja sent to their London address by some Kingston friends.

With few options available, Marley went to see Chris Blackwell, founder and head of Island, England's largest and most successful independent record company. To everyone's surprise, Blackwell advanced the Wailers the equivalent of about $20,000 to return to Jamaica and record a true album. He then spent another large sum of money to buy the Wailers out of their arrangement with Sims. He even allowed Tuff Gong to maintain the right to distribute the group's material in Jamaica. At last the Wailers had a record agreement that promised to be both creatively and financially profitable to them.

Most people in the music industry thought Blackwell had taken leave of his senses. No individual reggae artist or group had demonstrated the capability of selling an album in the British and American markets, which is where Blackwell intended to "break" the Wailers. Moreover, of all the Jamaican acts he could have chosen to work with, the Wailers had the reputation of being the most difficult. Friends and advisers, even other musicians, told Blackwell that he ought to kiss the money good-bye, that "those crazy Rastas" would return to Jamaica and that would be the last he would ever hear from them.

But Blackwell had very good reasons for his actions. A member of a prosperous Anglo-Jamaican family, he had spent much of his childhood in Jamaica and revered its culture and music. Moreover, as a teenager he had developed an enormous respect for Rastas when they came to his assistance after a boating accident left him hurt and stranded on a remote part of the island. He perceptively understood that Marley's Rasta beliefs and political convictions were essential to his greatness as an artist—and even purely from a marketing standpoint, he regarded them as a help rather than a hindrance.

To Blackwell, Marley was the real-life counterpart of the character Jimmy Cliff had played in *The Harder They Come*, a "rebel-type character" perfect for the rock music market. The record executive savvily recognized that "what Bob Marley believed in and how he lived his life was something that had tremendous appeal for the media. . . . Now here was this Third World superstar who had a different point of view, an individual against the system, who also had an incredible look: this was the first time you had seen anyone looking like that, other than Jimi Hendrix. And Bob had that power about him, and incredible lyrics." Given all this, Marley's reputation as "trouble," in Blackwell's words, bothered him not a bit: "In my experience when people are described like that, it usually just means that they know what they want."

The first true reggae album, *Catch a Fire*, was released in Great Britain in December 1972 and in the United States shortly thereafter. Though not initially an enormous seller, the album justified Blackwell's faith in the Wailers, garnering lavish praise from critics in both England and America. If some listeners in those countries were puzzled by this new Jamaican music, the sufferers had no trouble understanding the references in such songs as "Slave Driver," "400 Years," and "Concrete Jungle." Jamaican poet Linton Kwesi Johnson described

Catch a Fire as a landmark: "A whole new style of Jamaican music has come into being. It has a different character, a different sound . . . what I can only describe as 'International Reggae.' It incorporates elements from popular music, internationally: rock and soul, blues and funk."

To support the album, the Wailers toured Great Britain and the United States, another first for a reggae group. Though in the recent past they had played live in Jamaica only infrequently, years of rehearsing and recording together had made them a precision live act, one well able to live up to the underground word-of-mouth that preceded them. At London's Speakeasy Club, the aristocracy of the English rock world—Mick Jagger, Traffic, Bryan Ferry—turned out for the Wailers' sets and were not disappointed. "Bob had such charisma," said Mick Cater, who had been assigned by Island to help the group with its travel arrangements. "He was the best live act there's ever been, both with Peter and Bunny and later without them. A complete powerhouse onstage, but off, nothing like that, just very quiet."

But the warm reception the Wailers received was not sufficient to hide new tensions within the group. The unfamiliar grind of one-night stands in strange cities was especially wearing on Livingston, who was always unhappy anywhere but in Jamaica and often went days without eating when he could not get ital (unprocessed) food. Tosh, meanwhile, was growing uncomfortable with what he regarded as an increasing emphasis on Marley as the star, leader, and virtually sole songwriter of the group, which he believed was part of a conscious plan by Marley and Blackwell. Livingston and Tosh stayed on to record the group's second album, the uncompromising *Burnin'* in early 1973, but in June of that year Livingston announced he would not be part of the upcoming summer tour of the United States.

(As a solo artist, he then subsequently changed his name to Bunny Wailer.) His place was taken by Joe Higgs, and the Wailers played to enormous acclaim in various clubs in the Northeast, including Max's Kansas City in New York, where they opened for an up-and-coming singer named Bruce Springsteen.

By that time, *Burnin'* had been released. The album featured reworkings of old Wailers material such as "Small Axe" and "Duppy Conqueror" as well as new songs: immediate classics such as "I Shot the Sheriff," "Burnin' and Lootin,'" and "Rastaman Chant," an actual Rasta prayer sung to the accom-

The Wailers rehearse at an Island Records studio. Although the original trio had been as close as brothers, Bunny Livingston and Peter Tosh left Marley's group in 1973 because of creative tensions and the stress of constant touring.

paniment of burru drums. *Burnin'* was immediately hailed as a reggae masterpiece. It marked the end of the original Wailers, however. During the British club tour that followed at the end of 1973, the increasingly disgruntled Tosh left the group. Alluding to the Wailers' notorious dislike for cold weather, Island explained the cancellation of the remaining dates of the tour with a simple communiqué: "It snowed."

Though hurt by his friends' defection, Marley was also relieved. He had little stomach for the silent tension and angry outbursts that had characterized the trio's relationship while on the road. Never one to allow *anything* to interfere with his own creative drive, he was increasingly less willing to compromise in order to maintain group harmony.

From that point forward it would be Bob Marley *and* the Wailers, with no question as to who was the leader. Marley expanded the group's sound, adding to the Barretts, at various intervals, young keyboard wizards Earl "Wire" Lindo and Tyrone Downie, guitarists Al Anderson and Junior Marvin, his old friend Seeco Patterson on percussion, and the I-Threes—Rita Marley, Marcia Griffiths, and Judy Mowatt—on backing vocals. If reggae purists sometimes decried the rock tinge that the addition of the guitarists brought about, there was no denying that the revamped Wailers constituted an ensemble of unparalleled vocal and instrumental power. "One time I hear them say we finish with the tour," Family Man remembered about the troubles with Tosh and Livingston. "I think, 'Finish with it?' I think the tour just get started."

The new group was first heard on record in early 1975, when *Natty Dread* was released. The record was, in many ways, Marley's most outspoken yet, featuring such melodic, militant, poetic anthems as "Talkin' Blues," "Revolution," "Them Bellyful (But We Hungry)," and "Rebel Music," as well as the haunting, lovely "No Woman, No Cry."

Natty Dread was recorded over several months in 1974 in Jamaica, where Marley, having achieved a certain level of the success that had so long eluded him, relaxed into what for him constituted an almost settled way of life. While his wife and their four children lived in a modern house in the Rasta enclave at Bull Bay, 10 miles east of Kingston, he spent much of his time at Island House, the rambling home at 56 Hope Road, in a tony section of Kingston, that Chris Blackwell had sold to him.

There he occupied a small upstairs bedroom,

By 1972, Rita and Bob Marley had four children: (left to right) Sharon, David ("Ziggy"), Cedella, and Stephanie (in carriage).

unfurnished and undecorated except for a small mattress, a portrait of Haile Selassie on the wall, and his ever-present guitar. Various dreads and musicians were always in residence or coming and going from the house, as were one or another of Marley's lovers, who included the acclaimed Jamaican actress Esther Anderson; the women's table tennis champion of the Caribbean, Anita Belinais; and the stunningly beautiful Cindy Breakespeare, who would be voted Miss World for 1976. Sometimes Marley escaped with these companions to various hideaways he had around the island; his grandfather's house at Nine Miles also remained a refuge for him.

This "gypsy" aspect of Marley's personality, as a friend characterized it, was no secret to those close to him, including his wife: "It is something you learn to live with over a period of time," Rita Marley said. "I think Bob had such a lack of love when he was growing up. He seemed to be trying to prove to himself whether someone loved him and how much they loved him. There came a time when I had to say to him, 'If that's what you want, then I'll have to learn to live with it.' " Indeed, Rita opened her home to and helped raise many of the eight children that Marley fathered outside the marriage, all of whom he acknowledged and supported. Bob and Rita's daughter Cedella recalled that although her father was not constantly in residence at Bull Bay, "he was around," and that "it was kind of strict at home: you came home, you did your homework, and you went to bed." At 56 Hope Road, Marley maintained a similar kind of discipline. Able to function with very little sleep, he was unfailingly the last one to bed at night—Judy Mowatt remembers that "if you went to Bob's room at midnight, one o'clock, three o'clock, Bob would be playing a song"—and the first awake, usually with the sun. Most mornings, Alan Cole led Marley and company on a training run, a "little eye-opener," as Marley called it, that sometimes stretched out as long as 18 miles. Afterward, if there were no rehearsals or recording sessions scheduled, Marley liked to sit with his guitar on the steps of the back porch, one of his favorite spots for writing songs. Such days were always punctuated with the frequent sacramental intake of ganja, followed by the freewheeling, imaginative Rasta discussions known as "reasonings." And it was the rare afternoon that passed by without some kind of soccer game, the singer himself being a superb player of virtually professional caliber.

At some point Marley would meet with the

Throughout his life, Marley loved soccer almost as much as music. Exhibiting skills nearly equal to those of professional players, he took part in pickup games almost every day.

innumerable individuals who came to the house each day seeking his counsel. They included friends; fellow musicians; gunmen, rudies, and dreads from the ghetto; and poor people looking for help or money. According to Gilly Gilbert, the cook at the house who prepared such ital dishes as green banana porridge and fish head stew, "People come, hungry, and him try for help hungry people and poor people. Some him help, appreciate it, some no appreciate. . . . He try to help everyone, please everyone." Friends say that Marley sometimes gave away as much as $40,000 at such sessions.

Cindy Breakespeare confirmed that Marley's growing material success meant little to him. "He gave his dinner away," she said, adding that the only possessions that seemed to really matter to him were his guitar and the beloved jeans and boots that were his everyday apparel, even on stage. "People begged him things every day. Every day! He gave whatever to whoever. He didn't prize material things. And he didn't prize money. And he would always say that it was just passing through, so it wasn't important. . . . I think he felt that that was part of his role in life— to do for others and to give to others, and I think he felt very blessed because of the level of inspiration and the work that he had been called to do."

Despite his lack of interest in being a celebrity, *Natty Dread* catapulted Marley into true international superstardom. The way had been prepared the previous summer, when Eric Clapton's cover of "I Shot the Sheriff" became a monster hit in England and the United States. Marley and the "new" Wailers thus went out on the road in the summer of 1975 to a tumult of acclaim—interviews, magazine covers, sold-out shows at ever-larger venues in Great Britain and America. The five shows at the Lyceum Ballroom in London were recorded for a concert album, *Live*, which featured a particularly moving rendition of "No Woman, No

Cry" and succeeded in capturing the live power of the "Trench Town experience," the tag with which stage announcers sometimes introduced Marley and the Wailers.

Indeed, the magnitude of the emotions generated by Marley onstage could be overwhelming. A listener at one of Marley's concerts, wrote a critic for the *Washington Post*, "would have thought it was a political rally or a religious revival, not a pop concert . . . an apocalypse you can dance to." The first time she saw her son perform, in Philadelphia in 1976, Cedella Marley Booker was inspired to convert to Rastafari. Indeed, Marley and his fellow

At home among his people, Marley participates in a Rasta "reasoning" at Nine Miles. He especially enjoyed talking to passersby who appeared to be eccentric or mentally disturbed: "It's a mad man," he would excitedly exclaim. "Send him in for a reasoning."

musicians regarded themselves as missionaries, dedicated to spreading the truth of Jah Rastafari. "It was a crusade, it was a mission," remembers Judy Mowatt. "We were like sentinels, like lights. On tour the shows were like church: Bob delivering his sermon. There were mixed emotions in the audience: you see people literally crying, people in a frenzy, on a spiritual high. . . . There was a power that pulled you there. It was a clean feeling: you leave a concert as though you have learned something, have gained something."

Marley saw himself mainly as a peaceful "soul rebel." "Me only have one ambition," he asserted. "I only have one thing I really like to see happen. I like to see mankind live together—black, white, Chinese, everyone—that's all. . . . I don't come down on you really with blood and fire, earthquake and lightning, but you must know, see, that within me all that exists too." Despite the mellow, sinuous melodies, Marley's music expressed some of the righteous anger within, in his calls to "Stir It Up" and "Get Up, Stand Up (For Your Rights)." "When I remember the crack of the whip, my blood runs cold," he sang. "Slave driver, the table is turned / Catch a fire, you gonna get burned."

Such messages greatly unsettled Jamaica's political authorities. The government strongly urged the tourist board and other outlets to downplay Jamaica's association with reggae, Rasta, and especially Marley. "We obviously face a contradiction between the message of urban poverty and protest which reggae conveys and that of pleasure and relaxation inherent in our holiday product," read an internal Jamaica Tourist Board memo of October 10, 1975. "In short, when we promote reggae music we are promoting an aspect of Jamaican culture which is bound to draw attention to some of the harsher circumstances of our lives."

As these circumstances grew harsher, official

opposition to Marley intensified. The U.S. Central Intelligence Agency (CIA) designated him for their "most-watched" list in Jamaica, and the American ambassador informed the head of his British record label that the U.S. government was not happy about Marley, that "he was capable of destablising" the situation in the Caribbean. After the release of *Rastaman Vibration* in 1976, the Jamaican government formally banned four Marley songs—"War," "Crazy Baldheads," "Who the Cap Fit," and "Rat Race"—from the radio. As Marley became embroiled in the heightened election-year tensions, his life—like that of many prophets before him—became endangered by those who wished to silence his message of social justice.

In the previous national elections, held in 1972, Marley had openly supported the experiment in "democratic socialism" proposed by PNP leader Michael Manley. In contrast to the conservative JLP agenda, the PNP's program was more appealing to Marley and other Rastas in its emphasis on various social programs for the sufferers; socialism as opposed to capitalism as a means of redistributing wealth more fairly among the various levels of Jamaican society; restrictions on foreign exploitation of Jamaican resources; and a foreign policy that moved Jamaica closer toward Cuba and other Caribbean nations (many of them predominantly black) and further away from the United States. In addition, Manley had reached out to the Rasta community, receiving an audience with Haile Selassie and speaking positively of the Rastas' cultural influence.

By 1976 Marley's Rasta faith had become more militant. Disillusioned by Manley's failure to legalize ganja and by his creation of special courts that harshly dispensed summary justice to poor blacks, Marley was reluctant to support the PNP in its bid for reelection. Nonetheless, he was certainly more inclined toward the PNP, with its slogans of "Power to the People" and "Better Must Come," than he was to Edward Seaga's conservative JLP, which had the backing of the CIA. Specifying several conditions, Marley finally assented to the Manley government's request that he play a concert. The December 5 performance at the National Heroes Circle Stadium was to be a nonpolitical, nonpartisan event. With the free concert, Marley wished to thank Jamaicans for their support of his musical career, a gesture that he hoped would help bring the violent year to a peaceful close. It would be called the Smile Jamaica concert, after his latest single release, "Smile Jamaica," a lighthearted declaration of his pride in his Jamaican identity.

The Manley government agreed to Marley's conditions, but almost immediately after the singer announced his plans for the concert, the PNP declared that the upcoming national elections would be held 15 days later, on December 20. The closeness of the two dates made it appear as if Marley's Smile Jamaica concert was intended as an endorsement of the PNP. Now the threats that Marley had been receiving since his return home, warning him to get off the island and stay out of the election, increased in regularity.

As the day of the concert approached, the pressure mounted. A PNP vigilante squad set up a 24-hour armed guard outside Marley's home at 56 Hope Road. The security hardly made Marley, the Wailers, or the I-Threes feel safer as they proceeded with their daily rehearsals. At this point Marley was nearly as great an irritant to the PNP as he was to the JLP; perhaps the government would not mind if he were out of the way. Perhaps he was being set up; the authorities could always blame the JLP for any harm that came to him.

The constant tension undermined the Wailers' usual musical cohesiveness, and rehearsals proceeded fitfully. By late November, Marcia Griffiths, one of the I-Threes, had become so unnerved by the situation that she told Marley she could not perform with him and left Jamaica altogether. Another member of the trio, Judy Mowatt, was having ominous recurring dreams, which she interpreted as meaning that something awful was going to happen to Marley. Marley himself was haunted by a shadowy dream in which he was pursued by the sound of "pure gunshot."

At about nine o'clock on the night of December 3, Marley and the Wailers had just taken a short break from rehearsing. A ganja dealer had arrived, and Marley had stepped into the kitchen to eat a grapefruit. From the porch of 56 Hope Road, per-

The intense conflict between political factions in Jamaica is evident on this wall. Marley's radical message added to the tensions, which erupted in violence in 1976.

cussionist Seeco Patterson noticed, with some degree of concern, that the PNP vigilantes had disappeared. Suddenly two cars drove into the compound. Six gunmen exited the vehicles and began firing at the house with automatic weapons. Two of them burst inside, shooting wildly at anything that moved, and then the murderous entourage vanished into the night.

Seriously wounded in the attack was Marley's manager, Don Taylor, who took four bullets in the back and was pronounced dead at a Kingston hospital before being airlifted to Miami, Florida, for the surgery that saved his life. Rita Marley had her skull grazed by a bullet and was knocked unconscious. Marley himself was wounded in the chest and left arm. After being treated that night at a Kingston hospital, he retreated to a home in the Blue Mountains owned by Island Records chief Chris Blackwell.

There, in seclusion, guarded by a cadre of machete-wielding local Rastas, Marley pondered what to do while rumors about his condition and the identity and motives of his assailants swept the island. Adopting his protective screwface, Marley led those around him to believe that he was in doubt about whether to play the concert. "There's no way I'm going on stage without a machine gun," a friend remembered him saying. "Your guitar is your machine gun," the friend responded. Perhaps that reply helped Marley make up his mind, although Judy Mowatt believed that there was never any doubt about what he was going to do. "Bob was kind of iffy," she recalled, "but I knew that really his mind was already made up, because of the people. If it means his life, he would do it."

So on the night of December 5, the prophet came down from the mountain. Most of his band was still in hiding; Rita Marley, having just been released from the hospital, was waiting backstage still dressed in her hospital gown and bandages. Upon reaching the stadium, Marley was embraced by Manley and surrounded by a protective circle of 200 musicians and friends, offering themselves as human shields to the snipers possibly hiding among the otherwise ecstatic crowd of 80,000 people. It took Marley several minutes to quiet the roar that the throng sent up when it heard the stage announcer proclaim: "The great, the great, the great, the great Bob Marley!"

"When me decided to do this here concert two-and-a-half months ago," Marley said, "me was told there was no politics." He shook his dreadlocks in disgust. "I just wanted to play for the love of the people." Explaining that he was unable, because of his wounds, to play the guitar, he said he would sing just one song. Then he let loose an unearthly, reverberating wail, equal parts rebel cry and the screech of a jungle bird, that cued the pickup group of crack reggae musicians assembled onstage.

Shaking his mane of dreadlocks, bobbing up and down and dancing, feet together, in the movement he called the "rebel's hop," Marley brought his right hand to his temple and then extended it, forefinger first, toward his audience—a prophet's gesture, admonishing them to listen to what he had to say. Then he chanted as much as sang the opening words to a song from his most recent album, one that he had never played before an audience in his homeland. "What life has taught me," he sang, "I would like to share with those who want to learn."

He was "dancing in the spirit" now, said the I-Threes, who had long been convinced that when Marley was onstage he became entranced, virtually possessed. The backing vocalists regularly "saw spiritual things happen to Bob onstage that no one else was conscious of," Rita claimed. "Languages, Bob talking in tongues in his songs." He continued to chant as he spun around and around, dreadlocks whirling, his right forefinger pointing out to the audience, then up to the heavens, warning "that until the basic human rights / are guaranteed to all. . . . Until the philosophy which holds one race superior and another inferior / is finally discredited and abandoned—everywhere is war, me say war." The song was "War," Marley's musical adaptation of a speech on human rights given by Haile Selassie.

There was no containing Marley in the circle of protectors now, and any idea he had held about limiting himself to one song was quickly forgotten. For 90 mesmerizing minutes he continued, singing his "songs of freedom." At the end, still in the spirit, he rolled his left sleeve up and unbuttoned his shirt, triumphantly displaying his bullet wounds to the crowd. "You can't kill Jah," he had earlier sung; nor his messenger either, he now demonstrated. He crouched and put his hands at his hips, mimicking a gunfighter about to unholster his pistols. Then he drew, in the "bang-bang" gesture seemingly and sadly familiar to children everywhere, threw back his dreadlocks, and laughed. It sounded, said one who was on stage, "like a lion's roar." Then the prophet left the stage, and the next morning he left his own land. The exodus had begun. ◖◗

8

REDEMPTION SONGS

❧

IF THE GUNMEN and the authorities had thought they could silence Marley they were very much mistaken. After relocating to London and Miami, where he settled his wife, his children, and his mother, he produced two new albums that represented a reassessment, not retreat. *Exodus*, released in the summer of 1977, was Marley's biggest-selling album to date, remaining on the British charts for 56 weeks and yielding three smash singles—"Exodus," "Jammin'," and "Waiting in Vain," the last being one of Marley's finest love songs, written to Cindy Breakespeare. Other songs, such as "Guiltiness," were clearly inspired by the assassination attempt. The title cut reflected Marley's growing interest in Africa, both as the homeland of his ancestors and the literal and figurative promised land of his religion.

A European tour followed the album's release, but plans for American shows were canceled when the big toe on Marley's right foot was spiked during a pickup soccer game in Paris. He continued on with the European dates, but to his great annoyance, the wound grew extremely painful and refused to heal; at the end of a show, he often had to pour blood from his boot. A London doctor diagnosed the toe as cancerous and recommended amputation, but Marley refused and sought an alternate opinion. Rasta tenets forbade such procedures, he explained.

In the words of former Jamaican prime minister Michael Manley, Marley was "one of those extraordinary figures that . . . comes along once in a generation; who, starting with a folk art . . . by some inner magic of commitment, sincerity of passion and of just skill, turns it into a part of the universal language of the arts of the world."

"Rasta no abide amputation," he said. "I and I don't allow a man to be *dismantled*." A Miami physician suggested the less invasive procedure of a skin graft, to which Marley agreed.

The period of enforced rest that followed the procedure, spent mainly in Miami, inspired Marley's most reflective album, *Kaya* (another Jamaican word for marijuana), which was released in the spring of 1978. A series of lovely lilting hymns to the simple joys of life—sunshine, a misty morning, smoking ganja, making love—the record yielded one of Marley's hugest hits, "Is This Love?" Though some saw the album as a withdrawal from political concerns, Marley had always seen political struggle as the means to an end—the ability of individuals to live their life on earth joyfully. He explained,

> You can't show aggression all the while. To make music is a life that I have to live. Sometimes you have to fight with music. . . . But me always militant, you know. Me too militant. That's why me did things like *Kaya*, to cool off the pace. . . . I know when everything is cool and I know when I tremble, do you understand? Because music is something that everyone follows, so it's a force, a terrible force.

Further proof of the forcefulness of Marley's music and presence came in February 1978, when he returned to Jamaica for the first time since the attempt on his life. In his absence, political violence in Jamaica had escalated to such an extreme pitch that the ranking gunmen of the two opposition parties, Claudie Massop and Bucky Marshall, felt compelled to call upon the only man with the influence to bring about peace on the island: Bob Marley. When Marley's plane landed in Kingston on February 24, a huge crowd showered him with adoration, reminding many onlookers of Haile Selassie's dramatic visit 12 years earlier. Nearly two months later, on the very anniversary of that occasion, Marley gave a riveting performance at the One Love One Peace concert, which reached a dramatic conclusion when Marley persuaded political enemies Michael Manley and Edward Seaga to join hands onstage and pledge themselves to peace in Jamaica. Rarely had the ability of music to affect positive change been so tangibly demonstrated.

As the One Love One Peace concert demonstrated, Marley was ready to return to the stage. The world tour that followed was a succession of artistic and personal triumphs, its magnificence well documented on the live album *Babylon by Bus*. In the United States, as elsewhere, Marley was now playing larger venues than ever. The review of his June 1978 performance at Madison Square Garden by John Rockwell of the *New York Times* could have described the entire tour: "The concert was a triumph, for reggae in general but for Mr. Marley in particular. . . Mr. Marley was extraordinary. Who would have believed Madison Square Garden would have swayed *en masse* to a speech by Haile Selassie, the words of which Mr. Marley incorporates verbatim into 'War?' "

While in New York, Marley received one of his greatest honors from the combined African delegations to the United Nations, who presented the singer with the Third World Peace Medal "on behalf of five hundred million Africans" for his work for "equal rights and justice." Meeting the press afterward, Marley explained how his music served that cause: "When you fight revolution, you use guns. . . . Well, the music is the biggest gun, because it *save*. It no kill, right?" Earlier that year he had made his first visit to the fatherland, to Kenya and Ethiopia, where a relative of Haile Selassie's had given him a ring, with the figure of a lion on it, that once belonged to the emperor.

After shows in Europe, Marley and the Wailers

At the emotional conclusion of the 1978 One Love One Peace concert, Marley unites Jamaican political rivals Edward Seaga and Michael Manley. Marley viewed himself as "a revolutionary. . . . [who] fight it single-handed with music."

became the first reggae group to tour the Far East. In Japan, the group was stunned when the audience at each show sang along with every word of every song. Then in New Zealand, a delegation of Maoris, the island's native people, made a pilgrimage to Auckland, the country's capital, to officially welcome Marley. At a traditional native ceremony of greeting, they awarded him a name that translates as "the Redeemer."

Marley returned to the studio in the first months of 1979 to record the songs for *Survival*. The new album reflected his concern with African solidarity and independence. Marley was especially gratified to learn that one of its tracks, "Zimbabwe," was immediately adopted as the anthem of the black freedom fighters who were working to end decades of colonial and white rule in the former British colony of Rhodesia.

The following April Marley was invited to play at the ceremonies marking the official independence of the new nation of Zimbabwe. He would perform amid the ruins of Great Zimbabwe, a huge stone palace occupied by the kings of Zimbabwe before their nation was dominated by Britain. Marley was so gratified by the invitation that he paid the enormous expense of transporting his musicians and all their equipment to Zimbabwe. While he was awaiting a change of flights at Nairobi, Kenya, a messenger boarded Marley's plane with the information that Prince Charles of Great Britain, also on his way to the ceremonies in Zimbabwe, was in a nearby plane and would like Marley to come speak with him. "The prince want for see me," responded Marley in the best spirit of black independence, "him have for come here to me." Though the actual ceremonies were chaotic, resulting in an interruption of Marley's performance, he nevertheless regarded the event as the greatest honor of his career.

In May 1980 the Wailers embarked on their most ambitious tour yet, the Tuff Gong Uprising world tour. In six weeks in Europe, they played before more than one million fans in 12 different cities, marking them as the biggest concert attraction to that point in the continent's history. In Milan, Dublin, and London, the group performed outdoor shows before crowds of more than 100,000. The Milan show even outdrew a recent appearance by the pope.

The triumphant tour was marred only by the increasingly evident fatigue of its leader. Though Marley roused himself onstage night after night to give what many consider to be the most inspired performances of his career, offstage he was haggard,

Marley's eldest son, Ziggy, gets a special serenade. Years later, Ziggy followed in his father's footsteps by joining with some of his siblings to form the reggae group Ziggy Marley and the Melody Makers.

constantly exhausted, and more withdrawn than usual. Regularly accommodating to the press, as a means of spreading the message of Rastafari and reggae music, he now often deputed keyboardist Tyrone Downie to serve as his spokesman.

Most of those closest to Marley supposed that he was simply worn out, physically and emotionally, by the accumulated demands placed on him by family, friends, favor seekers, hangers-on, and his music. "He was just so pressured by people everywhere he went," recalls Cindy Breakespeare. "They were just drawn like moths to a flame, they couldn't stay away." Wailer Al Anderson was somewhat less charitable, describing the situation as "too many sharks on one piece of meat." The undeniable truth of such observations nonetheless failed to disclose the real cause of Marley's malaise.

The American leg of the Tuff Gong Uprising tour kicked off in September 1980. On September 21, the morning after he had played the second of two scheduled shows at Madison Square Garden in

New York, Marley went for a jog in Central Park with Alan Cole and some other friends. He had gone just a short distance, however, when he called out to Cole and collapsed, going into convulsions. Cole managed to get Marley back to his hotel, and while the band went on to Pittsburgh, site of their next gig two days later, physicians were consulted. The cancer from Marley's toe had spread throughout his body; the Tuff Gong had an inoperable brain tumor, and the doctors estimated that he would live for only two or three more weeks.

Marley proceeded to Pittsburgh, determined to play the next show. Band members vividly recall the immense sorrow of the sound check that day, when Marley sang over and over an early number called "Keep on Movin'," until its chorus of "Lord, I gotta keep on moving, Lord I gotta get on home" brought the I-Threes to tears and they asked him to stop. That night he and the band took the stage unannounced, Marley piercing the auditorium's darkness with his ululating rebel's trill. "Yeaaah!" he shouted. "Greetings in the name of His Imperial Majesty, Emperor Haile Selassie I, Jah, Rastafari, who liveth and reigneth in I and I I-tinually, ever faithful, ever sure." He then played an unforgettable set, climaxing in his first encore. Appropriately, "Redemption Song" was the last song on the last album released during Marley's lifetime, *Uprising*. That night onstage (as on the album) he played and sang it alone, picking out the beautiful melody on his battered acoustic guitar. "Won't you help me sing," he asked, "these songs of freedom, 'cause they're all I ever had—redemption songs; all I ever had, redemption songs, these songs of freedom, songs of freedom."

Backstage, the Wailers and the I-Threes were sobbing. "Now I realize what he went through," said Judy Mowatt. "Alone, because it had to be alone. We did not know how he was hurting. We did not

Approximately one million people, half of Jamaica's population, paid their respects as Marley's body was taken to its final resting place.

know the pain he was going through. We did not know if he was afraid. We did not know if he was wondering if he could do the show or not. He didn't say anything to anybody." Summoning the Wailers back to the stage for four more songs, Marley closed the concert, fittingly, with "Work," with its countdown of "five days to go. . . . four days to go . . ." When the show was over, he walked to the edge of the stage and shook hands with members of the audience.

Eight months later, on May 11, 1981, at the age of 36, as he had foreseen, Bob Marley died in Miami, Florida, after spending time in a New York City hospital and a West German clinic—whose director had been advised not to take him on as a patient, as he was "the most dangerous black man in the world." In different places in Kingston, Neville Garrick, Marcia Griffiths, and Judy Mowatt received the news of his death, they said, in the form of a lightning bolt and thunder crash, whose import they each immediately understood. Marley's funeral in Jamaica was attended by every important politician and dignitary in the country. More appropriately, an estimated one million people—virtually half the island's population—lined the roads in respect as his body was driven to its final resting place, a simple mausoleum next to the tiny shack where he grew up in Nine Miles.

Fifteen years after his death, Bob Marley's recordings remain classics, accounting for 40 percent of all the reggae music sold in the world. *Legend*, a Marley greatest-hits compilation, is one of the all-time best-selling albums in any musical category. Although Peter Tosh was murdered by robbers in 1987, Bunny Wailer and other musicians in the Wailers band continue to record. Marley's musical legacy is also carried on through the music of Ziggy Marley and the Melody Makers, composed of his children Ziggy, Sharon, Cedella, and Stephen.

Marley's greater political and spiritual message endures thoughout the world as well. An estimated half of the Jamaican population, as well as a huge proportion of the Jamaican immigrant population worldwide, pay allegiance to Jah Rastafari. At the end of the 1980s, a poll taken among African children revealed that Marley was the most revered figure on the continent, ahead even of such impressive figures as the South African freedom fighter Nelson Mandela. When sworn enemies Israel and the Palestine Liberation Organization (PLO) concluded a historic peace treaty in 1993, a giant billboard erected in Los Angeles—a city that is itself no stranger to seemingly intractable racial hatred and violence—to commemorate the event carried a huge photograph of Israeli leader Yitzhak Rabin and PLO chairman Yasser Arafat shaking hands. Above them was emblazoned the eternal question posed by

In Marley's old neighborhood of Trench Town, children play beneath a mural depicting the singer, Haile Selassie, and Jamaican activist Marcus Garvey.

Marley in "So Jah Seh": "If puss and dog can get together, why can't we love one another?"

"I perceive that his spirit is dancing all over the universe," said Judy Mowatt:

> His music has caused people all over the universe to be enlightened, to be happy, to be dancing. . . . So I would just look at it that his spirit is really dancing, touching all nationalities. . . . He is not gone, man: his work is here. He is alive. Whenever you call his name, you bring him alive. The reservoir of music he has left behind is like an encyclopedia: When you need to refer to a certain situation or crisis, there will always be a Bob Marley song that will relate to it. Bob was a musical prophet.

☙

APPENDIX:
SELECTED DISCOGRAPHY

Catch a Fire (1972)

Burnin' (1973)

Natty Dread (1974)

Live! (1974)

Rastaman Vibration (1976)

Exodus (1977)

Kaya (1978)

Babylon by Bus (1978)

Survival (1979)

Uprising (1980)

Confrontation (1983)

Legend (1984)

Rebel Music (1986)

Talkin' Blues (1991)

Songs of Freedom (1992)

Natural Mystic: Legend II (1995)

CHRONOLOGY

—— ❧ ——

1945   Born Nesta Robert Marley on February 6, in the parish of St. Ann, Jamaica

1959   Makes singing debut at a talent show; begins studying music with singer Joe Higgs

1961   Forms the Wailers with Bunny Livingston and Peter Tosh

1963   Auditions with the Wailers for producer Clement Dodd; the Wailers record "Simmer Down" with the Skatalites

1965   Songs by the Wailers occupy 5 of the top 10 slots on the Jamaican record charts; Marley begins romance with singer Rita Anderson

1966   Marley and Anderson are married. Ethiopian emperor Haile Selassie visits Jamaica; Marley and the Wailers convert to Rastafari; establish Wail 'N' Soul record label

1967   Wail 'N' Soul label fails; Bob and Rita Marley return to Nine Miles

1969   Marley writes and records for singer Johnny Nash and producer Leslie Kong; begins collaboration with Lee "Scratch" Perry and Aston "Family Man" Barrett

1971   Wailers establish the Tuff Gong production company; their first release, "Trench Town Rock," tops the Jamaican charts for five months; Wailers sign a contract with England's Island Records

1972   Island releases the Wailers' *Catch a Fire*, the first true reggae album

1973   The Wailers tour Great Britain and the United States; record their second album, *Burnin'*; Livingston and Tosh leave the group

1976   Jamaican government bans four songs from Marley's *Rastaman Vibration*; Marley is shot in an assassination attempt; performs at Smile Jamaica concert; leaves Jamaica to live in London and Miami

1977   *Exodus* remains on British charts for 56 weeks; Marley is diagnosed with cancer

1978   Returns to Jamaica to give the One Love One Peace concert; receives the Third World Peace Medal from the African delegations to the United Nations

1980   Attracts record crowds on the Tuff Gong Uprising world tour; collapses in New York and is diagnosed with inoperable cancer; plays his last concert in Pittsburgh

1981   Dies on May 11 in Miami

FURTHER READING

Barrett, Leonard. *The Rastafarians: Sounds of Cultural Dissonance*. Boston: Beacon, 1988.

Bob Marley. Book accompanying *Songs of Freedom* album release. Island Records Tuff Gong. 1992.

Boot, Adrian, and Chris Salewicz. *Bob Marley: Songs of Freedom*. New York: Viking Studio, 1995.

Davis, Stephen. *Bob Marley*. Rochester, Vermont: Schenkman, 1990.

Davis, Stephen, and Peter Simon. *Reggae Bloodlines: In Search of the Music and Culture of Jamaica*. New York: Da Capo, 1992.

Lazell, Barry. *Marley*. London: Hamlyn, 1994.

Talamon, Bruce, and Roger Steffens. *Bob Marley: Spirit Dancer*. New York: Norton, 1994.

Taylor, Don. *Marley and Me*. New York: Barricade Books, 1995.

White, Timothy. *Catch a Fire: The Life of Bob Marley*. New York: Henry Holt, 1992.

Whitney, Malika Lee, and Dermot Hussey. *Bob Marley: Reggae King of the World*. San Francisco: Pomegranate, 1994.

INDEX

SEAN DOLAN has a degree in literature and American history from SUNY Oswego. He is the author of many biographies and histories for young adult readers, including *James Beckwourth* and *Magic Johnson* in the Chelsea House BLACK AMERICANS OF ACHIEVEMENT series, and he has edited a series of volumes on the famous explorers of history.

NATHAN IRVIN HUGGINS, one of America's leading scholars in the field of black studies, helped select the titles for the BLACK AMERICANS OF ACHIEVEMENT series, for which he also served as senior consulting editor. He was the W. E. B. Du Bois Professor of History and of Afro-American Studies at Harvard University and the director of the W. E. B. Du Bois Institute for Afro-American Research at Harvard. He received his doctorate from Harvard in 1962 and returned there as a professor in 1980 after teaching at Columbia University, the University of Massachusetts, Lake Forest College, and the California State University, Long Beach. He was the author of four books and dozens of articles, including *Black Odyssey: The Afro-American Ordeal in Slavery*, *The Harlem Renaissance*, and *Slave and Citizen: The Life of Frederick Douglass*, and was associated with the Children's Television Workshop, National Public Radio, the Boston Athenaeum, the Museum of Afro-American History, the Howard Thurman Educational Trust, and Upward Bound. Professor Huggins died in 1989 at the age of 62 in Cambridge, Massachusetts.

PICTURE CREDITS